CROCK·POT®

◆ THE ORIGINAL SLOW COOKER ◆

favorite
slow cooker
recipes

Publications International, Ltd.

Pictured on the front cover: Smoky Chipotle Cassoulet *(page 50)*.

Pictured on the back cover (clockwise from left): Ham and Cheddar Brunch Strata *(page 14),* Meatballs and Spaghetti Sauce *(page 180)* and Rosemary Pork with Red Wine Risotto *(page 112)*.

ISBN-13: 978 1-4508-0247-5
ISBN-10: 1-4508-0247-8

Library of Congress Control Number: 2010925305

Manufactured in China.

8 7 6 5 4 3 2 1

Table of Contents

Joy of Slow Cooking

Slow Cooker Sizes

Smaller slow cookers—such as 1- to 3½-quart models—are the perfect size for cooking for singles, a couple, or empty-nesters (and also for serving dips).

While medium-size slow cookers (those holding somewhere between 3 quarts and 5 quarts) will easily cook enough food at a time to feed a small family, they're also convenient for holiday side dishes or appetizers.

Large slow cookers are great for large family dinners, holiday entertaining, and potluck suppers. A 6-quart to 7-quart model is ideal if you like to make meals in advance, or have dinner tonight and store leftovers for another day.

Types of Slow Cookers

Current **CROCK-POT**® slow cookers come equipped with many different features and benefits, from auto cook programs to stovetop-safe stoneware to timed programming. Visit **www.crockpot.com** to find the slow cooker that best suits your needs.

How you plan to use a slow cooker may affect the model you choose to purchase. For everyday cooking, choose a size large enough to serve your family. If you plan to use the slow cooker primarily for entertaining, choose one of the larger sizes. Basic slow cookers can hold as little as 16 ounces or as much as 7 quarts. The smallest sizes are great for keeping dips hot on a buffet, while the larger sizes can more readily fit large quantities of food and larger roasts.

Cooking, Stirring, and Food Safety

CROCK-POT® slow cookers are safe to leave unattended. The outer heating base may get hot as it cooks, but it should not pose a fire hazard. The heating element in the heating base functions at a low wattage and is safe for your countertops.

Your slow cooker should be filled about one-half to three-fourths full for most recipes unless otherwise instructed. Lean meats such as chicken or pork tenderloin will cook faster than meats with more connective tissue and fat such as beef chuck or pork shoulder. Bone-in meats will take longer than boneless cuts. Typical slow cooker dishes take approximately 7 to 8 hours to reach the simmer point on LOW and about 3 to 4 hours on HIGH. Once the vegetables and meat start to simmer and braise, their flavors will fully blend and meat will become fall-off-the-bone tender.

According to the USDA, all bacteria are killed at a temperature of 165°F. It is important to follow the recommended cooking times and not to open the lid often, especially early in the cooking process when heat is building up inside the unit. If you need to open the lid to check on your food or are adding additional ingredients, remember to allow additional cooking time if necessary to ensure food is cooked through and tender.

Oven-Safe

All **CROCK-POT®** slow cooker removable crockery inserts may (without their lids) be used safely in ovens at up to 400°F. Also, all **CROCK-POT®** slow cookers are microwavable without their lids. If you own another brand slow cooker, please refer to your owner's manual for specific crockery cooking medium tolerances.

Frozen Food

Frozen food or partially frozen food can be successfully cooked in a slow cooker; however, it will require longer cooking than the same recipe made with fresh food. It's almost always preferable to thaw frozen food prior to placing it in the slow cooker. Using an instant-read thermometer is recommended to ensure meat is fully cooked through.

Pasta and Rice

If you're converting a recipe that calls for uncooked pasta, cook the pasta on the stovetop just until slightly tender before adding to slow cooker. If you are converting a recipe that calls for cooked rice, stir in raw rice with other ingredients; add ¼ cup extra liquid per ¼ cup of raw rice.

Beans

Beans must be softened completely before combining with sugar and/or acidic foods. Sugar and acid have a hardening effect on beans and will prevent softening. Fully cooked canned beans may be used as a substitute for dried beans.

Vegetables

Root vegetables often cook more slowly than meat. Cut vegetables accordingly to cook at the same rate as meat—large or small, or lean versus marbled—and place near the sides or bottom of the stoneware to facilitate cooking.

Liquids

It is not necessary to use more than ½ to 1 cup liquid in most instances since juices in meats and vegetables are retained more in slow cooking than in conventional cooking. Excess liquid can be concentrated after slow cooking by removing meat and vegetables from stoneware, stirring in one of the following thickeners, and setting the slow cooker to HIGH. Cook on HIGH for approximately 15 minutes until juices are thickened.

Flour: All-purpose flour is often used to thicken soups or stews. Place flour in a small bowl or cup and stir in enough cold water to make a thin, lump-free mixture. With the slow cooker on HIGH, quickly stir the flour mixture into the liquid in the slow cooker. Cook, stirring frequently, until the mixture thickens.

Cornstarch: Cornstarch gives sauces a clear, shiny appearance; it is used most often for sweet dessert sauces and stir-fry sauces. Place cornstarch in a small bowl or cup and stir in cold water, stirring until the cornstarch dissolves. Quickly stir this mixture into the liquid in the slow cooker; the sauce will thicken as soon as the liquid boils. Cornstarch breaks down with too much heat, so never add it at the beginning of the slow cooking process, and turn off the heat as soon as the sauce thickens.

Arrowroot: Arrowroot (or arrowroot flour) comes from the root of a tropical plant that is dried and ground to a powder; it produces a thick clear sauce. Those who are allergic to wheat often use it in place of flour. Place arrowroot in a small bowl or cup and stir in cold water until the mixture is smooth. Quickly stir this mixture into the liquid in the slow cooker. Arrowroot thickens below the boiling point, so it even works well in a slow cooker on LOW. Too much stirring can break down an arrowroot mixture.

Tapioca: Tapioca is a starchy substance extracted from the root of the cassava plant. Its greatest advantage is that it withstands long cooking, making it an ideal choice for slow cooking. Add it at the beginning of cooking and you'll get a clear thickened sauce in the finished dish. Dishes using tapioca as a thickener are best cooked on the LOW setting; tapioca may become stringy when boiled for a long time.

Milk

Milk, cream, and sour cream break down during extended cooking. When possible, add during last 15 to 30 minutes of cooking, until just heated through. Condensed soups may be substituted for milk and can cook for extended times.

Fish

Fish is delicate and should be stirred in gently during the last 15 to 30 minutes of cooking time. Cook until just cooked through and serve immediately.

Baked Goods

If you wish to prepare bread, cakes, or pudding cakes in a slow cooker, you may want to purchase a covered, vented metal cake pan accessory for your slow cooker. You can also use any straight-sided soufflé dish or deep cake pan that will fit into the ceramic insert of your unit. Baked goods can be prepared directly in the insert; however, they can be a little difficult to remove from the insert, so follow the recipe directions carefully.

Easy
Entertaining

Hot Broccoli Cheese Dip

½ cup (1 stick) butter

6 stalks celery, sliced

2 onions, chopped

2 cans (4 ounces each) sliced mushrooms, drained

¼ cup plus 2 tablespoons all-purpose flour

2 cans (10¾ ounces each) condensed cream of celery soup

5 to 6 ounces garlic cheese, cut into cubes

2 packages (10 ounces each) frozen broccoli spears

French bread slices, bell pepper strips, cherry tomatoes

1. Melt butter in large skillet. Add celery, onions and mushrooms; cook and stir until translucent. Stir in flour and cook 2 to 3 minutes. Transfer to **CROCK-POT**® slow cooker.

2. Stir in soup, cheese and broccoli. Cover; cook on HIGH, stirring every 15 minutes, until cheese is melted. Turn **CROCK-POT**® slow cooker to LOW. Cover; cook 2 to 4 hours or until ready to serve.

3. Serve warm with bread slices and assorted vegetables.

Makes about 6 cups

PREP TIME: 10 to 15 minutes
COOK TIME: 30 minutes to 1 hour (HIGH) plus 2 to 4 hours (LOW)

Teriyaki Chicken Wings

3 to 4 pounds chicken wings

¼ cup soy sauce

¼ cup sherry

¼ cup honey

1 tablespoon hoisin sauce

1 tablespoon orange juice

2 cloves garlic, minced

1 fresh red chili pepper, finely chopped* (optional)

*Chili peppers can sting and irritate the skin, so wear rubber gloves when handling peppers and do not touch your eyes.

1. Place wings in **CROCK-POT**® slow cooker. Combine remaining ingredients in mixing bowl. Pour mixture over wings.

2. Cover; cook on LOW 3 to 3½ hours or on HIGH 1½ to 2 hours.

Makes 6 to 8 servings

PREP TIME: 10 minutes
COOK TIME: 3 to 3½ hours (LOW) or 1½ to 2 hours (HIGH)

Easy Entertaining

Oatmeal Crème Brûlée

4 cups water	2 cups whipping cream
3 cups quick-cooking oatmeal	1 teaspoon vanilla
½ teaspoon salt	¼ cup packed light brown sugar
6 egg yolks	Fresh berries (optional)
½ cup granulated sugar	

1. Coat **CROCK-POT**® slow cooker with nonstick cooking spray. Cover and preheat on HIGH to heat. Meanwhile, bring water to a boil. Immediately pour into preheated **CROCK-POT**® slow cooker. Stir in oatmeal and salt. Cover.

2. Combine egg yolks and granulated sugar in small bowl. Mix well; set aside. Heat cream and vanilla in medium saucepan over medium heat until mixture begins to simmer (small bubbles begin to form at edge of pan). Do not boil. Remove from heat. Whisk ½ cup hot cream into yolks, stirring rapidly so yolks don't cook.* Whisk warmed egg mixture into cream, stirring rapidly to blend well. Spoon mixture over oatmeal. Do not stir.

3. Turn **CROCK-POT**® slow cooker to LOW. Line lid with 2 paper towels. Cover tightly; cook on LOW 3 to 3½ hours or until custard has set.

4. Uncover and sprinkle brown sugar over surface of custard. Line lid with 2 dry paper towels. Cover tightly; continue cooking on LOW 10 to 15 minutes or until brown sugar has melted. Serve with fresh berries, if desired.

Makes 4 to 6 servings

*Place bowl on damp towel to prevent slipping.

Tip: This rich, sweet dish is delicious for breakfast or lunch, but also can be served as an unusual dessert.

PREP TIME: 15 minutes
COOK TIME: 3¼ to 3¾ hours (LOW)

Ham and Cheddar Brunch Strata

8 ounces French bread, torn into small pieces

2 cups shredded sharp Cheddar cheese, divided

1½ cups diced ham

½ cup finely chopped green onions (white and green parts), divided

4 large eggs

1 cup half-and-half or whole milk

1 tablespoon Worcestershire sauce

⅛ teaspoon ground red pepper

1. Coat **CROCK-POT**® slow cooker with nonstick cooking spray. Cut parchment paper to fit bottom of stoneware* and press into place. Spray paper lightly with nonstick cooking spray.

2. Layer in following order; bread, 1½ cups cheese, ham and all but 2 tablespoons green onions.

3. Whisk eggs, half-and-half, Worcestershire sauce and red pepper in small bowl. Pour evenly over layered ingredients in **CROCK-POT**® slow cooker. Cover; cook on LOW 3½ hours or until knife inserted into center comes out clean. Turn off heat. Sprinkle evenly with reserved ½ cup cheese and 2 tablespoons green onions. Let stand, covered, 10 minutes or until cheese has melted.

4. To serve, run a knife or rubber spatula around outer edges, lifting bottom slightly. Invert onto plate and peel off paper. Invert again onto serving plate.

Makes 6 to 8 servings

*To cut parchment paper to fit, trace around the stoneware bottom, then cut the paper slightly smaller to fit. If parchment paper is unavailable, substitute waxed paper.

PREP TIME: 30 minutes
COOK TIME: 3½ hours (LOW)

Artichoke and Nacho Cheese Dip

2 cans (10¾ ounces each) condensed nacho cheese soup, undiluted

1 can (14 ounces) quartered artichoke hearts, drained and coarsely chopped

1 cup (4 ounces) shredded or thinly sliced pepper jack cheese

1 can (4 ounces) evaporated milk

2 tablespoons minced chives, divided

½ teaspoon paprika

Crackers or chips

1. Combine soup, artichoke hearts, cheese, milk, 1 tablespoon chives and paprika in **CROCK-POT**® slow cooker. Cover; cook on LOW 2 hours.

2. Stir well. Sprinkle with remaining 1 tablespoon chives and serve with crackers.

Makes about 1 quart

PREP TIME: 5 minutes
COOK TIME: 2 hours (LOW)

Asian-Spiced Chicken Wings

3 pounds chicken wings	¼ cup dry sherry
1 cup packed brown sugar	½ cup hoisin sauce
1 cup soy sauce	1 tablespoon fresh lime juice
½ cup ketchup	3 tablespoons sesame seeds, toasted
2 teaspoons fresh ginger, minced	
2 cloves garlic, minced	¼ cup green onions, thinly sliced

1. Broil the chicken wings 10 minutes on each side or until browned. Transfer chicken wings to **CROCK-POT**® slow cooker. Add next 6 ingredients; stir thoroughly. Cover; cook on LOW 5 to 6 hours or on HIGH 2 to 3 hours or until wings are no longer pink, stirring once halfway through the cooking time to baste the wings with sauce.

2. Remove wings from stoneware. Remove ¼ cup of cooking liquid (discard the rest). Combine reserved liquid with hoisin sauce and lime juice. Drizzle mixture over wings.

3. Before serving, sprinkle wings with sesame seeds and green onions.

Makes 10 to 16 wings

Note: Chicken wings are always crowd pleasers. Garnishing them with toasted sesame seeds and green onions gives these appetizers added crunch and contrasting color.

Tip: For 5-, 6- or 7-quart **CROCK-POT**® slow cooker, increase chicken wings to 5 pounds.

PREP TIME: 25 minutes
COOK TIME: 5 to 6 hours (LOW) or 2 to 3 hours (HIGH)

Chocolate-Stuffed Slow Cooker French Toast

6 slices (¾-inch-thick) day-old
   challah*

½ cup semisweet chocolate chips,
   divided

6 eggs

3 cups half-and-half

⅔ cup granulated sugar

1 teaspoon vanilla

¼ teaspoon salt

   Powdered sugar or warm
    maple syrup

   Fresh fruit (optional)

*Challah is usually braided. If you use
brioche or another rich egg bread, slice
bread to fit baking dish.

1. Generously butter 2½-quart baking dish that fits inside **CROCK-POT**® slow cooker. Arrange 2 bread slices in bottom of dish. Sprinkle on ¼ cup chocolate chips. Add 2 more bread slices. Sprinkle with remaining ¼ cup chocolate chips. Top with remaining 2 bread slices.

2. Beat eggs in large bowl. Stir in half-and-half, granulated sugar, vanilla and salt. Pour egg mixture over bread layers. Press bread into liquid. Set aside 10 minutes or until bread has absorbed liquid. Cover dish with buttered foil, butter-side down.

3. Pour 1 inch hot water into **CROCK-POT**® slow cooker. Add baking dish. Cover; cook on HIGH 3 hours or until toothpick inserted into center comes out clean. Remove dish and let stand 10 minutes to firm up. Serve with powdered sugar. Garnish with fresh fruit, if desired.

Makes 6 servings

Tip: Any oven-safe casserole or baking dish is safe to use in your **CROCK-POT**® slow cooker. Place directly inside the stoneware, and follow the recipe directions.

PREP TIME: 15 minutes
COOK TIME: 3 hours (HIGH)

Asian Barbecue Skewers

2 pounds boneless, skinless chicken thighs

½ cup soy sauce

⅓ cup packed brown sugar

2 tablespoons sesame oil

3 cloves garlic, minced

½ cup thinly sliced scallions

1 tablespoon toasted sesame seeds (optional)

1. Cut each thigh into 4 pieces about 1½ inches thick. Thread chicken onto 7-inch-long wooden skewers, folding thinner pieces, if necessary. Place skewers into **CROCK-POT®** slow cooker, layering as flat as possible.

2. Combine soy sauce, brown sugar, oil and garlic in small bowl. Reserve ⅓ cup sauce; set aside. Pour remaining sauce over skewers. Cover; cook on LOW 2 hours. Turn skewers over and cook 1 hour longer.

3. Transfer skewers to serving platter. Discard cooking liquid. Spoon on reserved sauce and sprinkle with sliced scallions and sesame seeds, if desired.

Makes 4 to 6 servings

PREP TIME: 10 minutes
COOK TIME: 3 hours (LOW)

Cuban-Style Curried Turkey

4 tablespoons all-purpose flour

1 teaspoon salt, or to taste

½ teaspoon black pepper, or to taste

2 pounds turkey breast meat, cut into 1-inch cubes*

4 tablespoons vegetable oil, divided

2 small onions, chopped

2 cloves garlic, minced

2 cans (14½ ounces each) diced tomatoes, undrained

2 cans (15 ounces each) black beans, rinsed and drained

1 cup chicken broth

⅔ cup raisins

½ teaspoon curry powder

¼ teaspoon crushed red pepper flakes

Juice of 1 lime (2 tablespoons)

2 tablespoons minced fresh cilantro

2 tablespoons minced green onion, green part only

4 cups cooked rice (optional)

*You may substitute turkey tenderloins; cut as directed.

1. Combine flour, salt and pepper in resealable plastic food storage bag. Add turkey cubes and shake well to coat. Heat 2 tablespoons oil in large skillet over medium heat until hot. Add turkey and brown on all sides in batches, about 5 minutes per batch. Transfer to **CROCK-POT**® slow cooker.

2. Heat remaining 2 tablespoons oil in skillet. Add onions and cook and stir over medium heat 3 minutes or until golden. Stir in garlic and cook an additional 30 seconds. Transfer to **CROCK-POT**® slow cooker.

3. Stir in tomatoes with juice, beans, broth, raisins, curry powder and red pepper flakes. Cover; cook on LOW 1 hour. Stir in lime juice. Sprinkle with cilantro and green onion. Adjust seasonings, if desired. Serve over rice, if desired.

Makes 8 servings

PREP TIME: 15 minutes
COOK TIME: 1 hour (LOW)

Cheesy Shrimp on Grits

1 cup finely chopped green bell pepper

1 cup finely chopped red bell pepper

½ cup thinly sliced celery

1 bunch green onions, chopped, divided

4 tablespoons (½ stick) butter, cubed

1¼ teaspoons seafood seasoning

2 bay leaves

¼ teaspoon ground red pepper

1 pound uncooked shrimp, peeled, deveined and cleaned

5⅓ cups water

1⅓ cups quick-cooking grits

8 ounces shredded sharp Cheddar cheese

¼ cup whipping cream or half-and-half

1. Coat **CROCK-POT**® slow cooker with nonstick cooking spray. Add bell peppers, celery, all but ½ cup green onions, butter, seafood seasoning, bay leaves and red pepper. Cover; cook on LOW 4 hours or on HIGH 2 hours.

2. Turn **CROCK-POT**® slow cooker to HIGH. Add shrimp. Cover; cook 15 minutes longer. Meanwhile, bring water to a boil in medium saucepan. Add grits and cook according to directions on package.

3. Discard bay leaves from shrimp mixture. Stir in cheese, cream and remaining ½ cup green onions. Cook 5 minutes longer or until cheese has melted. Serve over grits.

Makes 6 servings

Tip: Seafood is delicate and should be added to the **CROCK-POT**® slow cooker during the last 15 to 30 minutes of the cooking time on HIGH, and during the last 30 to 45 minutes on the LOW setting. Seafood overcooks easily, so watch your cooking times, and cook only until seafood is done.

PREP TIME: 15 minutes
COOK TIME: 4 hours (LOW) or 2 hours (HIGH) plus 15 minutes (HIGH

Pork Roast Landaise

2	tablespoons olive oil	¼	cup red wine vinegar
2½	pounds boneless, center-cut pork loin roast	¼	cup sugar
	Salt and black pepper, to taste	½	cup port or sherry wine
1	medium onion, diced	2	cups chicken broth, divided
2	large cloves garlic, minced	2	tablespoons cornstarch
2	teaspoons dried thyme	3	pears, cored and sliced ¾-inch thick
2	parsnips, cut into ¾-inch slices	1½	cups pitted prunes

1. Heat olive oil in large saucepan over medium-high heat. Season pork roast with salt and pepper; brown roast on all sides in saucepan. Place roast in **CROCK-POT®** slow cooker.

2. Add onion and garlic to saucepan. Cook and stir over medium heat 2 to 3 minutes. Stir in thyme. Transfer to **CROCK-POT®** slow cooker. Add parsnips; stir well.

3. Combine vinegar and sugar in same saucepan. Cook over medium heat, stirring constantly, until mixture thickens into syrup. Add port and cook 1 minute more. Add 1¾ cups chicken broth. Combine remaining ¼ cup of broth with cornstarch in small bowl. Whisk in cornstarch mixture, and cook until smooth and slightly thickened. Pour into **CROCK-POT®** slow cooker.

4. Cover; cook on LOW 8 hours or on HIGH 4 hours. Add pears and prunes during last 30 minutes of cooking.

Makes 4 to 6 servings

PREP TIME: 30 minutes
COOK TIME: 8 hours (LOW) or 4 hours (HIGH)

Easiest Three-Cheese Fondue

2 cups (8 ounces) shredded mild or sharp Cheddar cheese

¾ cup reduced-fat (2%) milk

½ cup (2 ounces) crumbled blue cheese

1 package (3 ounces) cream cheese, cut into cubes

¼ cup finely chopped onion

1 tablespoon all-purpose flour

1 tablespoon butter or margarine

2 cloves garlic, minced

4 to 6 drops hot pepper sauce

⅛ teaspoon ground red pepper

Breadsticks and assorted fresh vegetables for dipping

1. Combine all ingredients except breadsticks and vegetables in **CROCK-POT**® slow cooker. Cover; cook on LOW 2 to 2½ hours, stirring once or twice, until cheese is melted and smooth.

2. Increase heat to HIGH. Cook 1 to 1½ hours or until heated through. Serve with breadsticks and fresh vegetables for dipping.

Makes 8 servings

Tip: To reduce the total fat in this recipe, use reduced-fat Cheddar cheese and Neufchâtel cheese instead of full-fat cream cheese.

PREP TIME: 10 minutes
COOK TIME: 2 to 2½ hours (LOW) plus 1 to 1½ hours (HIGH)

Honey-Mustard Chicken Wings

3 pounds chicken wings
1 teaspoon salt
1 teaspoon black pepper
½ cup honey

½ cup barbecue sauce
2 tablespoons spicy brown mustard
1 clove garlic, minced
3 to 4 thin lemon slices

1. Preheat broiler. Cut off wing tips; discard. Cut each wing at joint to make 2 pieces. Season with salt and pepper. Place on broiler pan. Broil 4 to 5 inches from heat about 5 minutes per side. Transfer to **CROCK-POT**® slow cooker.

2. Combine honey, barbecue sauce, mustard and garlic in small bowl; mix well. Pour sauce over chicken wings. Top with lemon slices. Cover; cook on LOW 4 to 5 hours. Before serving, remove and discard lemon slices. Serve wings with sauce.

Makes 4 to 5 appetizer servings

PREP TIME: 30 minutes
COOK TIME: 4 to 5 hours (LOW)

Pepperoni Pizza Dip with Breadstick Dippers

1 jar or can (14 ounces) pizza
  sauce
¾ cup chopped turkey
  pepperoni
4 green onions, chopped
1 can (2¼ ounces) sliced black
  olives, drained

½ teaspoon dried oregano
1 cup (4 ounces) shredded
  mozzarella cheese
1 package (3 ounces) cream
  cheese, softened
Breadstick Dippers (recipe
  follows)

1. Combine pizza sauce, pepperoni, green onions, olives and oregano in 2-quart **CROCK-POT**® slow cooker. Cover; cook on LOW 2 hours or on HIGH 1 to 1½ hours or until mixture is hot.

2. Stir in mozzarella and cream cheese until melted and well blended. Serve with warm breadsticks.

Makes 8 servings

PREP TIME: 20 minutes
COOK TIME: 2 hours (LOW) or 1 to 1½ hours (HIGH)

Breadstick Dippers

1 package (8 ounces)
  refrigerated breadstick
  dough

2 teaspoons melted butter
2 teaspoons minced parsley

Bake breadsticks according to package directions. Brush with melted butter and sprinkle with parsley. Serve with warm dip.

Wild Rice and Dried Cherry Risotto

1 cup dry-roasted salted peanuts

2 tablespoons sesame oil, divided

1 cup chopped onion

6 ounces uncooked wild rice

1 cup diced carrots

1 cup chopped green or red bell pepper

½ cup dried cherries

⅛ to ¼ teaspoon red pepper flakes

4 cups hot water

¼ cup teriyaki or soy sauce

1 teaspoon salt, or to taste

1. Coat **CROCK-POT**® slow cooker with nonstick cooking spray. Heat large skillet over medium-high heat until hot. Add peanuts. Cook and stir 2 to 3 minutes or until peanuts begin to brown. Transfer peanuts to plate; set aside.

2. Heat 2 teaspoons oil in skillet until hot. Add onion. Cook and stir 6 minutes or until richly browned. Transfer to **CROCK-POT**® slow cooker.

3. Stir in wild rice, carrots, bell pepper, cherries, pepper flakes and water. Cover; cook on HIGH 3 hours.

4. Let stand 15 minutes, uncovered, until rice absorbs liquid. Stir in teriyaki sauce, peanuts, remaining oil and salt.

Makes 8 to 10 servings

PREP TIME: 5 minutes
COOK TIME: 3 hours (HIGH)

Pork Chops with Dried Fruit and Onions

6 bone-in end-cut pork chops
   (about 2½ pounds)
   Salt and black pepper, to taste
3 tablespoons vegetable oil
2 onions, diced
2 cloves garlic, minced

¼ teaspoon dried sage
¾ cup quartered pitted dried
   plums
¾ cup chopped mixed dried fruit
3 cups unsweetened, unfiltered
   apple juice
1 bay leaf

1. Season pork chops with salt and pepper. Heat oil in large skillet over medium-high heat until hot. Sear pork on both sides to brown, cooking in batches, if necessary. Transfer to **CROCK-POT**® slow cooker.

2. Add onions to hot skillet. Cook and stir over medium heat until softened. Add garlic and cook 30 seconds more. Sprinkle sage over mixture. Add dried plums, mixed fruit and apple juice. Bring mixture to a boil. Reduce heat and simmer, uncovered, 3 minutes, scraping bottom and sides of pan to release browned bits. Ladle mixture over pork chops.

3. Add bay leaf. Cover; cook on LOW 3½ to 4 hours, or until pork chops are tender. Remove bay leaf. Add salt and pepper, if desired. To serve, spoon fruit and cooking liquid over pork chops.

Makes 6 servings

PREP TIME: 20 minutes
COOK TIME: 3½ to 4 hours (LOW)

Warm and Spicy Fruit Punch

4 cinnamon sticks

1 orange, washed

1 square (8 inches) double-thickness cheesecloth

1 teaspoon whole allspice

½ teaspoon whole cloves

7 cups water

1 can (12 ounces) frozen cran-raspberry juice concentrate, thawed

1 can (6 ounces) frozen lemonade concentrate, thawed

2 cans (5½ ounces each) apricot nectar

1. Break cinnamon into pieces. Using vegetable peeler, remove strips of orange peel. Squeeze juice from orange; set juice aside.

2. Rinse cheesecloth; squeeze out water. Wrap cinnamon, orange peel, allspice and cloves in cheesecloth. Tie bag securely with cotton string or strip of cheesecloth.

3. Combine reserved orange juice, water, concentrates and apricot nectar in **CROCK-POT**® slow cooker; add spice bag. Cover; cook on LOW 5 to 6 hours. Remove and discard spice bag before serving.

Makes about 14 servings

Tip: To keep punch warm during a party, place your **CROCK-POT**® slow cooker on the buffet table, and turn the setting to LOW or WARM.

PREP TIME: 15 minutes
COOK TIME: 5 to 6 hours (LOW)

Korean Barbecue Beef

4 to 4½ pounds beef short ribs

¼ cup chopped green onions (white and green parts)

¼ cup tamari or soy sauce

¼ cup beef broth or water

1 tablespoon packed brown sugar

2 teaspoons minced fresh ginger

2 teaspoons minced garlic

½ teaspoon black pepper

2 teaspoons dark sesame oil

Hot cooked rice or linguine pasta

2 teaspoons sesame seeds, toasted

1. Place ribs in **CROCK-POT**® slow cooker. Combine green onions, tamari, broth, brown sugar, ginger, garlic and pepper in medium bowl; mix well and pour over ribs. Cover; cook on LOW 7 to 8 hours or until ribs are fork-tender.

2. Remove ribs from cooking liquid. Cool slightly. Trim excess fat and discard. Cut rib meat into bite-size pieces, discarding bones and fat.

3. Let cooking liquid stand 5 minutes to allow fat to rise. Skim off fat and discard.

4. Stir sesame oil into cooking liquid. Return beef to **CROCK-POT**® slow cooker. Cover; cook on LOW 15 to 30 minutes or until hot. Serve over rice; garnish with sesame seeds.

Makes 6 servings

Tip: Three pounds of boneless short ribs can be substituted for the beef short ribs.

PREP TIME: 20 minutes
COOK TIME: 7 to 8 hours (LOW)

Herbed Turkey Breast with Orange Sauce

1 large onion, chopped

3 cloves garlic, minced

1 teaspoon dried rosemary

½ teaspoon black pepper

1 boneless, skinless turkey breast (2 to 3 pounds)

1½ cups orange juice

1. Place onion in **CROCK-POT**® slow cooker. Combine garlic, rosemary and pepper in small bowl; set aside.

2. Cut slices about three-fourths of the way through turkey at 2-inch intervals. Rub garlic mixture between slices. Place turkey, cut side up, in **CROCK-POT**® slow cooker. Pour orange juice over turkey. Cover; cook on LOW 7 to 8 hours.

3. Serve sliced turkey with orange sauce.

Makes 4 to 6 servings

Tip: Don't peek! The **CROCK-POT**® slow cooker can take as long as 30 minutes to regain heat lost when the cover is removed. Only remove the cover when instructed to do so by the recipe.

PREP TIME: 20 minutes
COOK TIME: 7 to 8 hours (LOW)

Easy Entertaining

44

Maple-Glazed Meatballs

1½ cups ketchup

1 cup maple syrup or maple-flavored syrup

⅓ cup reduced-sodium soy sauce

1 tablespoon quick-cooking tapioca

1½ teaspoons ground allspice

1 teaspoon dry mustard

2 packages (about 16 ounces each) frozen fully cooked meatballs, partially thawed and separated

1 can (20 ounces) pineapple chunks in juice, drained

1. Combine ketchup, maple syrup, soy sauce, tapioca, allspice and mustard in **CROCK-POT®** slow cooker.

2. Carefully stir meatballs and pineapple chunks into ketchup mixture.

3. Cover; cook on LOW 5 to 6 hours. Stir before serving. Serve warm; insert cocktail picks, if desired.

Makes about 48 meatballs

Tip: For a quick main dish, serve meatballs over hot cooked rice.

PREP TIME: 15 minutes
COOK TIME: 5 to 6 hours (LOW)

Risotto-Style Peppered Rice

1 cup uncooked converted long-grain rice

1 medium green bell pepper, chopped

1 medium red bell pepper, chopped

1 cup chopped onion

½ teaspoon ground turmeric

⅛ teaspoon ground red pepper (optional)

1 can (14½ ounces) fat-free chicken broth

4 ounces Monterey Jack cheese with jalapeño peppers, cubed

½ cup milk

¼ cup (½ stick) butter, cut into small pieces

1 teaspoon salt

1. Place rice, bell peppers, onion, turmeric and ground red pepper, if desired, in **CROCK-POT**® slow cooker. Stir in broth. Cover; cook on LOW 4 to 5 hours or until rice is tender and broth is absorbed.

2. Stir in cheese, milk, butter and salt; fluff rice with fork. Cover; cook on LOW 5 minutes or until cheese melts.

Makes 4 to 6 servings

Tip: Dairy products should be added at the end of the cooking time because they will curdle if cooked in the **CROCK-POT**® slow cooker for a long time.

PREP TIME: 10 to 15 minutes
COOK TIME: 4 to 5 hours (LOW)

Smoky Chipotle Cassoulet

1 pound boneless, skinless chicken thighs, cubed

1 teaspoon salt

1 teaspoon ground cumin

1 bay leaf

1 chipotle pepper in adobo sauce, minced

1 medium onion, diced

1 can (15 ounces) navy beans, rinsed and drained

1 can (15 ounces) black beans, rinsed and drained

1 can (14½ ounces) crushed tomatoes, undrained

1½ cups chicken stock

½ cup fresh-squeezed orange juice

¼ cup chopped fresh cilantro (optional)

1. Combine all ingredients except cilantro in **CROCK-POT®** slow cooker. Cover; cook on LOW 7 to 8 hours or on HIGH 4 to 5 hours.

2. Remove bay leaf before serving. Garnish with cilantro, if desired.

Makes 6 servings

PREP TIME: 10 minutes
COOK TIME: 7 to 8 hours (LOW) or 4 to 5 hours (HIGH)

Apricot and Brie Dip

½ cup dried apricots, finely chopped

⅓ cup plus 1 tablespoon apricot preserves, divided

¼ cup apple juice

1 (2-pound) brie, rind removed, cut into cubes

Bread rusks, crackers or crudité for dipping

Combine dried apricots, ⅓ cup apricot preserves and apple juice in **CROCK-POT**® slow cooker. Cover and cook on HIGH 40 minutes. Stir in brie and cook 30 to 40 minutes longer or until melted. Stir in remaining 1 tablespoon preserves. Turn **CROCK-POT**® slow cooker to LOW and serve with bread rusks, crackers or crudité.

Makes 8 to 12 servings

PREP TIME: 10 minutes
COOK TIME: 1 hour 10 minutes to 1 hour 50 minutes (HIGH)

Gratin Potatoes with Asiago Cheese

6 slices bacon, cut into 1-inch
   pieces
6 medium baking potatoes,
   peeled and thinly sliced

½ cup grated Asiago cheese
   Salt and black pepper, to taste
1½ cups heavy cream

1. Heat skillet over medium heat until hot. Add bacon. Cook and stir until crispy. Transfer to paper towel-lined plate with slotted spoon to drain.

2. Pour bacon fat from skillet into **CROCK-POT**® slow cooker. Layer one fourth of potatoes on bottom of **CROCK-POT**® slow cooker. Sprinkle one fourth of bacon over potatoes and top with one fourth of cheese. Add salt and pepper to taste. Repeat layers using remaining ingredients. Pour cream over all. Cover; cook on LOW 7 to 9 hours or on HIGH 5 to 6 hours. Adjust salt and pepper, if desired.

Makes 4 to 6 servings

PREP TIME: 15 minutes
COOK TIME: 7 to 9 hours (LOW) or 5 to 6 hours (HIGH)

Soups
and Stews

Hearty Lentil and Root Vegetable Stew

2 cans (about 14 ounces each) chicken broth

1½ cups turnips, cut into 1-inch cubes

1 cup dried red lentils, rinsed and sorted

1 medium onion, cut into ½-inch wedges

2 medium carrots, cut into 1-inch pieces

1 medium red bell pepper, cut into 1-inch pieces

½ teaspoon dried oregano

⅛ teaspoon red pepper flakes

1 tablespoon olive oil

½ teaspoon salt

4 slices bacon, crisp-cooked and crumbled

½ cup finely chopped green onions

1. Combine broth, turnips, lentils, onion, carrots, bell pepper, oregano and pepper flakes in **CROCK-POT**® slow cooker. Stir to mix well. Cover; cook on LOW 6 hours or on HIGH 3 hours, or until lentils are tender.

2. Stir in olive oil and salt. Sprinkle each serving with bacon and green onion.

Makes 8 servings

PREP TIME: 15 minutes
COOK TIME: 6 hours (LOW) or 3 hours (HIGH)

Butternut Squash-Apple Soup

3 packages (12 ounces each)
  frozen cooked winter squash,
  thawed and drained or about
  4½ cups mashed cooked
  butternut squash

2 cans (about 14 ounces each)
  chicken broth

1 medium Golden Delicious
  apple, peeled, cored and
  chopped

2 tablespoons minced onion

1 tablespoon packed brown
  sugar

1 teaspoon minced fresh sage or
  ½ teaspoon ground sage

¼ teaspoon ground ginger

½ cup whipping cream or half-
  and-half

1. Combine squash, broth, apple, onion, brown sugar, sage and ginger in
CROCK-POT® slow cooker.

2. Cover; cook on LOW 6 hours or on HIGH 3 hours or until squash is tender.

3. Purée soup in food processor or blender. Stir in cream just before serving.

Makes 6 to 8 servings

Tip: For thicker soup, use only 3 cups chicken broth.

PREP TIME: 15 minutes
COOK TIME: 6 hours (LOW) or 3 hours (HIGH)

Soups and Stews

Easy Corn Chowder

2 cans (14½ ounces each)
   chicken broth

1 bag (16 ounces) frozen corn,
   thawed

3 small red potatoes, peeled and
   cut into ½-inch pieces

1 red bell pepper, diced

1 medium onion, diced

1 stalk celery, sliced

½ teaspoon salt

½ teaspoon black pepper

¼ teaspoon ground coriander

½ cup heavy cream

8 slices bacon, crisp-cooked and
   crumbled

1. Place broth, corn, potatoes, bell pepper, onion, celery, salt, black pepper and coriander into **CROCK-POT**® slow cooker. Cover; cook on LOW 7 to 8 hours.

2. Partially mash soup mixture with potato masher to thicken. Stir in cream; cook on HIGH, uncovered, until hot. Adjust seasonings, if desired. To serve, sprinkle on bacon.

Makes 6 servings

Tip: Defrost meat and vegetables before cooking them in the **CROCK-POT**® slow cooker.

PREP TIME: 15 minutes
COOK TIME: 7 to 8 hours (LOW)

Northwest Beef and Vegetable Soup

2 tablespoons olive oil

1 pound lean stew beef, fat removed and cut into 1-inch cubes

1 medium onion, chopped

1 clove garlic, minced

3½ cups canned crushed tomatoes, undrained

1 can (15 ounces) white beans, drained and rinsed

1 buttercup squash, peeled and diced

1 turnip, peeled and diced

1 large potato, peeled and diced

2 stalks celery, sliced

2 tablespoons minced fresh basil

1½ teaspoons salt

1 teaspoon black pepper

8 cups water

1. Heat oil in skillet over medium heat until hot. Sear beef on all sides, turning as it browns. Add onion and garlic during last few minutes of searing. Transfer to **CROCK-POT**® slow cooker.

2. Add remaining ingredients. Gently stir well to combine. Cover; cook on HIGH 2 hours. Turn **CROCK-POT**® slow cooker to LOW. Cook on LOW 4 to 6 hours longer, stirring occasionally and adjusting seasonings to taste.

Makes 6 to 8 servings

PREP TIME: 20 minutes
COOK TIME: 2 hours (HIGH) plus 4 to 6 hours (LOW)

Asian Beef Stew

2 onions, cut into ¼-inch slices

1½ pounds round steak, sliced thin across the grain

2 stalks celery, sliced

2 carrots, peeled and sliced or 1 cup peeled baby carrots

1 cup sliced mushrooms

1 cup orange juice

1 cup beef broth

⅓ cup hoisin sauce

2 tablespoons cornstarch

1 to 2 teaspoons Chinese five-spice powder or curry powder

1 cup frozen peas

Hot cooked rice

Chopped fresh cilantro (optional)

1. Place onions, beef, celery, carrots and mushrooms in **CROCK-POT**® slow cooker.

2. Combine orange juice, broth, hoisin sauce, cornstarch and five-spice powder in small bowl. Pour into **CROCK-POT**® slow cooker. Cover; cook on HIGH 5 hours or until beef is tender.

3. Stir in peas. Cook 20 minutes longer or until peas are tender. Serve with hot cooked rice, and garnish with cilantro, if desired.

Makes 6 servings

PREP TIME: 10 minutes
COOK TIME: 5½ hours (HIGH)

Cannellini Minestrone Soup

4 cups chicken broth

1 can (14½ ounces) diced tomatoes, undrained

1 can (12 ounces) tomato-vegetable juice

2 cups escarole, cut into ribbons

1 cup chopped green onions

1 cup chopped carrots

1 cup chopped celery

1 cup chopped potatoes

¼ cup dried cannellini beans, sorted and rinsed

2 tablespoons chopped fresh chives

1 tablespoon chopped fresh flat-leaf parsley

¼ teaspoon salt

¼ teaspoon black pepper

2 ounces uncooked ditalini pasta

1. Place all ingredients except pasta in **CROCK-POT**® slow cooker. Stir well to combine. Cover; cook on LOW 6 to 8 hours or on HIGH 4 to 6 hours.

2. Add ditalini and stir again. Cover; cook 20 minutes before serving.

Makes 6 servings

PREP TIME: 15 minutes
COOK TIME: 6 to 8 hours (LOW) or 4 to 6 hours (HIGH)

Cheesy Tavern Soup

4 tablespoons olive oil

½ cup chopped celery

½ cup chopped carrot

½ cup chopped onion

½ cup chopped green bell pepper

2 quarts chicken broth

2 cans (12 ounces each) beer, at room temperature

4 tablespoons (½ stick) butter

2 teaspoons salt

2 teaspoons black pepper

½ cup all-purpose flour

4 cups (16 ounces) shredded Cheddar cheese

1. Heat oil in skillet over medium heat until hot. Add celery, carrot, onion and bell pepper. Cook and stir until tender. Transfer to **CROCK-POT**® slow cooker.

2. Add broth, beer, butter, salt and pepper. Cover; cook on LOW 6 hours or on HIGH 2 to 4 hours.

3. Dissolve flour in small amount of water. Add to **CROCK-POT**® slow cooker, stirring in well. Continue cooking 10 to 15 minutes or until thickened.

4. To serve, preheat broiler. Ladle soup into individual broiler-safe bowls. Top each with ½ cup grated cheese. Broil 10 to 15 minutes or until cheese has melted.

Makes 8 servings

PREP TIME: 15 minutes

COOK TIME: 6 hours (LOW) or 2 to 4 hours (HIGH)

Black Bean Chipotle Soup

1 pound dry black beans

2 stalks celery, cut into ¼-inch dice

2 carrots, cut into ¼-inch dice

1 yellow onion, cut into ¼-inch dice

2 chipotle peppers in adobo sauce, chopped

1 cup crushed tomatoes

1 can (4 ounces) chopped mild green chilies, drained

6 cups chicken or vegetable stock

2 teaspoons cumin

Salt and black pepper, to taste

Optional toppings: sour cream, chunky-style salsa, fresh chopped cilantro

1. Rinse and sort beans and place in large bowl; cover completely with water. Soak 6 to 8 hours or overnight. (To quick-soak beans, place beans in large saucepan; cover with water. Bring to a boil over high heat. Boil 2 minutes. Remove from heat; let soak, covered, 1 hour.) Drain beans; discard water.

2. Place beans in **CROCK-POT**® slow cooker. Add celery, carrots and onion.

3. Combine chipotles, tomatoes, chilies, stock and cumin in medium bowl. Add to **CROCK-POT**® slow cooker. Cover; cook on LOW 7 to 8 hours or on HIGH 4½ to 5 hours, or until beans are tender. Season with salt and pepper.

4. If desired, process mixture in blender, in 2 or 3 batches, to desired consistency, or leave chunky. Serve with sour cream, salsa and cilantro, if desired.

Makes 4 to 6 servings

Tip: For an even heartier soup, add 1 cup diced browned spicy sausage, such as linguiça or chouriço.

PREP TIME: 20 minutes
COOK TIME: 7 to 8 hours (LOW) or 4½ to 5 hours (HIGH)

Manhattan Clam Chowder

3 slices bacon, diced

2 stalks celery, chopped

3 onions, chopped

2 cups water

1 can (15 ounces) stewed tomatoes, undrained and chopped

4 small red potatoes, diced

2 carrots, diced

½ teaspoon dried thyme

½ teaspoon black pepper

½ teaspoon Louisiana-style hot sauce

1 pound minced clams*

*If fresh clams are unavailable, use canned clams; 6 (6½-ounce) cans yield about 1 pound of clam meat; drain and discard liquid.

1. Cook and stir bacon in medium saucepan until bacon is crisp. Remove bacon and place in **CROCK-POT**® slow cooker.

2. Add celery and onions to skillet. Cook and stir until tender. Place in **CROCK-POT**® slow cooker.

3. Mix in water, tomatoes with juice, potatoes, carrots, thyme, pepper and hot sauce. Cover; cook on LOW 6 to 8 hours or HIGH 4 to 6 hours. Add clams during last half hour of cooking.

Makes 4 servings

Tip: Shellfish and mollusks are delicate and should be added to the **CROCK-POT**® slow cooker during the last 15 to 30 minutes of the cooking time if you're using the high heat setting, and during the last 30 to 45 minutes if you're using the low setting. This type of seafood overcooks easily, becoming tough and rubbery, so watch your cooking times, and cook only long enough for foods to be done.

PREP TIME: 10 minutes
COOK TIME: 6 to 8 hours (LOW) or 4 to 6 hours (HIGH)

Chorizo Chili

1 pound 90% lean ground beef

8 ounces bulk raw chorizo or ½ package (15 ounces) raw chorizo

1 can (16 ounces) chili beans in chili sauce

2 cans (14½ ounces) zesty chili-style diced tomatoes, undrained

1. Place beef and chorizo in **CROCK-POT**® slow cooker. Break up with fork to form small chunks.

2. Stir in beans and tomatoes and juice. Cover; cook on LOW 7 hours. Skim off and discard excess fat before serving.

Makes 6 servings

Serving suggestion: Top with sour cream or shredded cheese.

PREP TIME: 5 minutes
COOK TIME: 7 hours (LOW)

Black and White Chili

1 pound chicken tenders, cut into ¾-inch pieces

1 cup coarsely chopped onion

1 can (about 15 ounces) Great Northern beans, drained

1 can (about 15 ounces) black beans, drained

1 can (about 14 ounces) Mexican-style stewed tomatoes, undrained

2 tablespoons Texas-style chili powder seasoning mix

1. Spray large skillet with cooking spray; heat over medium heat until hot. Add chicken and onion; cook and stir 5 minutes or until chicken is browned.

2. Combine chicken mixture, beans, tomatoes with juice and chili seasoning in **CROCK-POT**® slow cooker. Cover; cook on LOW 4 to 4½ hours.

Makes 6 servings

Serving Suggestion: For a change of pace, this delicious chili is excellent served over cooked rice or pasta.

PREP TIME: 10 minutes
COOK TIME: 4 to 4½ hours (LOW)

Linguiça & Green Bean Soup

1 large yellow onion, chopped

3 cloves garlic, minced

2 tablespoons olive oil

1 cup tomato juice

4 cups water

1 tablespoon Italian seasoning

2 teaspoons garlic salt

1 teaspoon ground cumin

1 bay leaf

2 cans (16 ounces each) cut green beans, drained

1 can (16 ounces) kidney beans, drained

1 pound linguiça sausage, fried until cooked through then cut into bite-sized pieces

1. Place all ingredients in **CROCK-POT**® slow cooker. Cover; cook on LOW 8 to 10 hours or on HIGH 4 to 6 hours. Add more boiling water during cooking, if necessary.

2. Serve with warm cornbread.

Makes 6 servings

PREP TIME: 20 minutes
COOK TIME: 8 to 10 hours (LOW) or 4 to 6 hours (HIGH)

Hearty Meatball Stew

3 pounds ground beef or
   ground turkey

1 cup Italian bread crumbs

4 eggs

½ cup milk

¼ cup grated Romano cheese

2 teaspoons salt

2 teaspoons garlic salt

2 teaspoons black pepper

2 tablespoons olive oil

2 cups water

2 cups beef broth

1 can (14½ ounces) stewed
   tomatoes, undrained

1 can (12 ounces) tomato paste

1 cup chopped carrots

1 cup chopped onions

¼ cup chopped celery

1 tablespoon Italian seasoning

1. Combine beef, bread crumbs, eggs, milk, cheese, salt, garlic salt and pepper in large bowl. Form into 2-inch-round balls. Heat oil in skillet over medium-high heat until hot. Brown meatballs on all sides. Transfer to **CROCK-POT**® slow cooker.

2. Add remaining ingredients. Stir well to combine. Cover; cook on LOW 4 to 6 hours or on HIGH 2 to 4 hours.

Makes 6 to 8 servings

PREP TIME: 20 minutes
COOK TIME: 4 to 6 hours (LOW) or 2 to 4 hours (HIGH)

Irish Stew

1 cup fat-free, reduced-sodium chicken broth	1 pound lean lamb for stew, cut into 1-inch cubes
1 teaspoon dried marjoram	8 ounces frozen cut green beans, thawed
1 teaspoon dried parsley flakes	2 small leeks, cut lengthwise into halves, then crosswise into slices
¾ teaspoon salt	
½ teaspoon garlic powder	
¼ teaspoon black pepper	1½ cups coarsely chopped carrots
1¼ pounds white potatoes, peeled and cut into 1-inch pieces	

1. Combine broth, marjoram, parsley, salt, garlic powder and pepper in large bowl; mix well. Transfer to **CROCK-POT**® slow cooker.

2. Layer potatoes, lamb, green beans, leeks and carrots into **CROCK-POT**® slow cooker. Cover; cook on LOW 7 to 9 hours or until lamb is tender.

Makes 6 servings

Tip: If desired, thicken cooking liquid with a mixture of 1 tablespoon cornstarch and ¼ cup water. Stir mixture into cooking liquid; cook on HIGH 10 to 15 minutes or until thickened.

PREP TIME: 5 minutes
COOK TIME: 7 to 9 hours (LOW)

Soups and Stews

Jerk Pork and Sweet Potato Stew

2	tablespoons all-purpose flour	1	clove garlic, minced
¼	teaspoon salt, or to taste	½	medium scotch bonnet chile or jalapeño pepper, cored, seeded and minced (about 1 teaspoon)*
¼	teaspoon black pepper, or to taste		
1¼	pounds pork shoulder, cut into bite-size pieces	⅛	teaspoon ground allspice
2	tablespoons vegetable oil	1	cup chicken broth
1	large sweet potato, peeled and diced	1	tablespoon lime juice
		2	cups cooked rice (optional)
1	cup frozen or canned corn		
¼	cup minced green onions, green parts only, divided		

*Scotch bonnet chiles and jalapeño peppers can sting and irritate the skin, so wear rubber gloves when handling and do not touch your eyes.

1. Combine flour, salt and pepper in resealable plastic food storage bag. Add pork and shake well to coat. Heat oil in large skillet over medium heat until hot. Add pork in a single layer (working in 2 batches, if necessary) and brown on both sides, about 5 minutes. Transfer to **CROCK-POT**® slow cooker.

2. Add sweet potato, corn, 2 tablespoons green onions, garlic, chile and allspice. Stir in broth. Cover; cook on LOW 5 to 6 hours.

3. Stir in lime juice and remaining 2 tablespoons green onions. Adjust salt and pepper to taste. Serve stew over cooked rice, if desired.

Makes 4 servings

Tip: To reduce the amount of fat in **CROCK-POT**® slow cooker meals, trim excess fat from meats and degrease canned broth before using.

PREP TIME: 15 minutes
COOK TIME: 5 to 6 hours (LOW)

Caramelized French Onion Soup

4 extra-large sweet onions,
   peeled
4 tablespoons (½ stick) butter
2 cups dry white wine
8 cups beef or vegetable broth,
   divided

2 cups water
1 tablespoon minced fresh
   thyme
6 slices French bread, toasted
1 cup shredded Swiss or Gruyère
   cheese

1. Cut each onion into quarters. Cut each quarter into ¼-inch-thick slices. Heat skillet over medium heat until hot. Add butter and onions. Cook until soft and caramel brown, about 45 to 50 minutes, stirring every 7 to 8 minutes. Transfer to **CROCK-POT**® slow cooker.

2. Add wine to skillet and let liquid reduce to about ½ cup, simmering about 15 minutes. Transfer to **CROCK-POT**® slow cooker.

3. Add broth, water and thyme to **CROCK-POT**® slow cooker. Cover; cook on HIGH 2½ hours or until thoroughly heated.

4. To serve, ladle soup into individual ovenproof soup bowls. Float one slice of toast in each bowl and sprinkle with cheese. Preheat oven broiler and place bowls on top shelf of oven. Broil 3 to 5 minutes, or until cheese is melted and golden. Serve immediately.

Makes 6 servings

PREP TIME: 1¼ hours
COOK TIME: 2½ hours (LOW)

Italian Hillside Garden Soup

1 tablespoon extra-virgin olive oil

1 cup chopped green bell pepper

1 cup chopped onion

½ cup sliced celery

1 can (14½ ounces) diced tomatoes with basil, garlic and oregano, undrained

1 can (15½ ounces) navy beans, drained and rinsed

1 medium zucchini, chopped

1 cup frozen cut green beans, thawed

2 cans (14 ounces each) chicken broth

¼ teaspoon garlic powder

1 package (9 ounces) refrigerated sausage- or cheese-filled tortellini pasta

3 tablespoons chopped fresh basil

Grated Asiago or Parmesan cheese (optional)

1. Heat oil in large skillet over medium-high heat until hot. Add bell pepper, onion and celery. Cook and stir 4 minutes or until onions are translucent. Transfer to **CROCK-POT**® slow cooker.

2. Add tomatoes with juice, navy beans, zucchini, green beans, broth and garlic powder. Cover; cook on LOW 7 hours or on HIGH 3½ hours.

3. Turn **CROCK-POT**® slow cooker to HIGH. Add tortellini and cook 20 to 25 minutes longer or until pasta is tender. Stir in basil. Garnish each serving with cheese.

Makes 6 servings

Tip: Cooking times are guidelines. **CROCK-POT**® slow cookers, just like ovens, cook differently depending on a variety of factors, including capacity. For example, cooking times will be longer at higher altitudes.

PREP TIME: 15 minutes
COOK TIME: 7½ hours (LOW) or 4 hours (HIGH)

Hearty Chicken Tequila Soup

1 small onion, cut into 8 wedges

1 cup frozen corn, thawed

1 can (14½ ounces) diced tomatoes with mild green chilies, undrained

2 cloves garlic, minced

2 tablespoons chopped fresh cilantro, plus additional for garnish

1 whole fryer chicken (about 3½ pounds)

2 cups chicken broth

3 tablespoons tequila

¼ cup sour cream

1. Spread onions on bottom of **CROCK-POT**® slow cooker. Add corn, tomatoes, garlic and 2 tablespoons cilantro. Mix well to combine. Place chicken on top of tomato mixture.

2. Combine broth and tequila in medium bowl. Pour over chicken and tomato mixture. Cover; cook on LOW 8 to 10 hours.

3. Transfer chicken to cutting board. Remove skin and bones. Pull meat apart with 2 forks into bite-size pieces. Return chicken to **CROCK-POT**® slow cooker and stir.

4. Serve with dollop of sour cream and garnish with cilantro.

Makes 2 to 4 servings

PREP TIME: 10 minutes
COOK TIME: 8 to 10 hours (LOW)

Golden Harvest Pork Stew

1 pound boneless pork cutlets, cut into 1-inch pieces

2 tablespoons all-purpose flour, divided

1 tablespoon vegetable oil

2 medium Yukon gold potatoes, unpeeled and cut into 1-inch cubes

1 large sweet potato, peeled and cut into 1-inch cubes

1 cup chopped carrots

1 ear corn, broken into 4 pieces or ½ cup corn

½ cup chicken broth

1 jalapeño pepper, seeded and finely chopped*

1 clove garlic, minced

1 teaspoon salt

¼ teaspoon black pepper

¼ teaspoon dried thyme

Chopped parsley

*Jalapeño peppers can sting and irritate the skin, so wear rubber gloves when handling peppers and do not touch eyes.

1. Toss pork pieces with 1 tablespoon flour; set aside. Heat oil in large skillet over medium-high heat until hot. Add pork; cook until browned on all sides. Transfer to **CROCK-POT**® slow cooker.

2. Add remaining ingredients, except parsley and 1 tablespoon flour. Cover; cook on LOW 5 to 6 hours.

3. Combine remaining 1 tablespoon flour and ¼ cup cooking liquid from stew in small bowl; stir until smooth. Stir flour mixture into stew. Cook on HIGH 10 minutes or until thickened. To serve, sprinkle with parsley.

Makes 4 servings

PREP TIME: 20 minutes
COOK TIME: 5 to 6 hours (LOW)

Creamy Farmhouse Chicken and Garden Soup

½ package (16 ounces) frozen pepper stir-fry vegetable mix

1 cup frozen corn

1 medium zucchini, sliced

2 bone-in chicken thighs, skinned

½ teaspoon minced garlic

1 can (14 ounces) fat-free chicken broth

½ teaspoon dried thyme

2 ounces uncooked egg noodles

1 cup half-and-half

½ cup frozen green peas, thawed

2 tablespoons chopped parsley

2 tablespoons butter

1 teaspoon salt

½ teaspoon coarsely ground black pepper

1. Coat **CROCK-POT**® slow cooker with nonstick cooking spray. Place stir-fry vegetables, corn and zucchini in bottom. Add chicken, garlic, broth and thyme. Cover; cook on HIGH 3 to 4 hours or until chicken is no longer pink in center. Remove chicken and set aside to cool slightly.

2. Add noodles to **CROCK-POT**® slow cooker. Cover; cook 20 minutes longer, or until noodles are done.

3. Meanwhile, debone and chop chicken. Return to **CROCK-POT**® slow cooker. Stir in remaining ingredients. Let stand 5 minutes before serving.

Makes 4 servings

Note: To skin chicken easily, grasp skin with paper towel and pull away. Repeat with fresh paper towel for each piece of chicken, discarding skins and towels.

PREP TIME: 15 minutes
COOK TIME: 3½ to 4½ hours (LOW)

Hearty Chicken Chili

- 1 medium onion, finely chopped
- 1 small jalapeño pepper, cored, seeded and minced*
- 1 small clove garlic, minced
- 1½ teaspoons medium-hot chili powder
- ¾ teaspoon salt, or to taste
- ½ teaspoon black pepper, or to taste
- ½ teaspoon ground cumin
- ½ teaspoon crushed dried oregano
- 2 cans (15½ ounces each) hominy, drained and rinsed
- 1 can (15 ounces) pinto beans, drained and rinsed
- 1½ pounds boneless, skinless chicken thighs, cut into 1-inch pieces
- 1 cup chicken broth
- 1 tablespoon all-purpose flour (optional)

  Chopped parsley or cilantro, for garnish

*Jalapeño peppers can sting and irritate the skin, so wear rubber gloves when handling peppers and do not touch eyes. For a hotter dish, add ¼ teaspoon crushed red pepper flakes with the seasonings.

1. Combine onion, jalapeño, garlic, chili powder, salt, pepper, cumin, and oregano in **CROCK-POT**® slow cooker.

2. Add hominy, beans, chicken and broth. Stir well to combine. Cover; cook on LOW 7 hours.

3. If thicker gravy is desired, combine 1 tablespoon flour and 3 tablespoons cooking liquid in small bowl. Add to **CROCK-POT**® slow cooker. Cover; cook on HIGH 10 minutes, or until thickened. Serve in bowls and garnish as desired.

Makes 6 servings

PREP TIME: 15 minutes
COOK TIME: 7 hours (LOW)

Lamb Shank and Mushroom Stew

2 tablespoons olive oil, divided

2 large lamb shanks (about 2 pounds total)

2 tablespoons all-purpose flour

2 cups sliced mushrooms*

1 small red onion, thinly sliced

1 large clove garlic, minced

1¼ cups chicken broth

½ cup pitted sliced green olives

¼ teaspoon salt, or to taste

⅛ teaspoon black pepper, or to taste

⅛ teaspoon crushed dried thyme

2 tablespoons capers

4 cups cooked noodles

*Shiitake mushroom caps are preferred for this dish, but you may use other mushroom varieties, if necessary.

1. Heat 1 tablespoon oil in large skillet over medium-high heat until hot. Dust lamb shanks with flour, reserving leftover flour. Brown lamb on all sides, about 3 minutes per side. Transfer to **CROCK-POT**® slow cooker.

2. Heat remaining 1 tablespoon oil in skillet over medium-high heat until hot. Add mushrooms, onion and garlic. Cook and stir 3 minutes or until vegetables are tender. Transfer mixture to **CROCK-POT**® slow cooker.

3. Sprinkle reserved flour into skillet and stir. Pour chicken broth into skillet. Stir to scrape up any browned bits. Continue to cook and stir 2 minutes longer or until mixture is slightly thickened. Pour into **CROCK-POT**® slow cooker.

4. Stir in olives, salt, pepper and thyme. Cover; cook on LOW 7 to 8 hours or on HIGH 4 to 5 hours.

5. Transfer lamb to cutting board. Gently pull lamb meat from bones with fork. Discard bones. Let cooking liquid stand 5 minutes. Skim off and discard excess fat. Return lamb to **CROCK-POT**® slow cooker. Stir in capers. Adjust seasoning, if desired. Serve lamb and sauce over noodles.

Makes 4 servings

PREP TIME: 30 minutes
COOK TIME: 7 to 8 hours (LOW) or 4 to 5 hours (HIGH)

Hamburger Veggie Soup

1 pound 95% lean ground beef

1 bag (16 ounces) frozen mixed vegetables

1 package (10 ounces) frozen seasoning-blend vegetables

1 can (10¾ ounces) condensed tomato soup, undiluted

1 can (14½ ounces) stewed tomatoes, undrained

2 cans (5½ ounces each) spicy vegetable juice

Salt and black pepper, to taste

Coat **CROCK-POT**® slow cooker with nonstick cooking spray. Crumble beef before placing in bottom. Add remaining ingredients. Stir well to blend. Cover; cook on HIGH 4 hours. If necessary, break up large pieces of beef. Add salt and pepper before serving, if desired.

Makes 4 to 6 servings

PREP TIME: 5 minutes
COOK TIME: 4 hours (HIGH)

Cioppino

1 pound cod, halibut or any
   firm-fleshed white fish, cubed
1 cup sliced mushrooms
2 carrots, sliced
1 onion, chopped
1 green pepper, chopped
1 teaspoon minced garlic
1 can (15 ounces) tomato sauce
1 can (14 ounces) beef broth

1 teaspoon salt
½ teaspoon black pepper
½ teaspoon dried oregano
1 can (7 ounces) cooked clams
½ pound cooked shrimp
1 package (6 ounces) cooked
   crabmeat
   Minced fresh parsley

1. Combine fish pieces, mushrooms, carrots, onion, green pepper, garlic, tomato sauce, broth, salt, black pepper and oregano in **CROCK-POT**® slow cooker. Cover; cook on LOW 10 to 12 hours.

2. Turn **CROCK-POT**® slow cooker to HIGH. Add clams, shrimp and crabmeat. Cover; cook on HIGH 30 minutes or until seafood is heated through. Garnish with parsley before serving.

Makes 6 servings

PREP TIME : 20 to 30 minutes
COOK TIME: 10 to 12 hours (LOW) plus 30 minutes (HIGH)

Creative
Cooking

Warm Blue Crab Bruschetta

4 cups peeled, seeded and diced
    Roma or plum tomatoes

1 cup diced white onion

2 teaspoons minced garlic

⅓ cup olive oil

2 tablespoons balsamic vinegar

½ teaspoon dried oregano

2 tablespoons sugar

1 pound lump blue crabmeat,
    picked over for shells

1½ teaspoons kosher salt

½ teaspoon cracked black
    pepper

⅓ cup minced fresh basil

2 baguettes, sliced and toasted

1. Combine tomatoes, onion, garlic, oil, vinegar, oregano and sugar in **CROCK-POT**® slow cooker. Cover; cook on LOW 2 hours.

2. Add crabmeat, salt and pepper. Stir gently to mix, taking care not to break up crabmeat lumps. Cook on LOW 1 hour.

3. Fold in basil. Serve on toasted baguette slices.

Makes 16 servings

Serving Suggestion: Crab topping can also be served on Melba toast or whole-grain crackers.

PREP TIME: 20 minutes
COOK TIME: 3 hours (LOW)

Winter Squash and Apples

1 teaspoon salt

½ teaspoon black pepper

1 butternut squash (about 2 pounds), peeled and seeded

2 apples, cored and cut into slices

1 medium onion, quartered and sliced

1½ tablespoons butter

1. Combine salt and pepper in small bowl; set aside.

2. Cut squash into 2-inch pieces; place in **CROCK-POT**® slow cooker. Add apples and onion. Sprinkle with salt mixture; stir well. Cover; cook on LOW 6 to 7 hours or until vegetables are tender.

3. Just before serving, stir in butter and season to taste with additional salt and pepper.

Makes 4 to 6 servings

PREP TIME: 15 minutes
COOK TIME: 6 to 7 hours (LOW)

Creative Cooking

Provençal Lemon and Olive Chicken

2 cups chopped onion

8 skinless chicken thighs (about 2½ pounds)

1 lemon, thinly sliced and seeds removed

1 cup pitted green olives

1 tablespoon olive brine from jar or white vinegar

2 teaspoons herbes de Provence

1 bay leaf

½ teaspoon salt

⅛ teaspoon black pepper

1 cup chicken broth

½ cup minced fresh parsley

1. Place onion in **CROCK-POT**® slow cooker. Arrange chicken thighs over onion. Place lemon slice on each thigh. Add olives, brine, herbes de Provence, bay leaf, salt and pepper. Slowly pour in chicken broth.

2. Cover; cook on LOW 5 to 6 hours or on HIGH 3 to 3½ hours or until chicken is tender. Stir in parsley before serving.

Makes 8 servings

Note: To skin chicken easily, grasp skin with paper towel and pull away. Repeat with fresh paper towel for each piece of chicken, discarding skins and towels.

PREP TIME: 20 minutes
COOK TIME: 5 to 6 hours (LOW) or 3 to 3½ hours (HIGH)

Steamed Pork Buns

½ container (18 ounces) refrigerated cooked shredded pork in barbecue sauce*

1 tablespoon Asian garlic chili sauce

1 container (16.3 ounces) refrigerated big biscuits (8 biscuits)

Dipping Sauce (recipe follows)

Sliced green onions, for garnish

*Look for pork in plain, not smoky, barbecue sauce. Substitute chicken in barbecue sauce, if desired.

1. Combine pork and chili sauce in medium bowl. Split biscuits in half. Roll or stretch each biscuit into 4-inch circle. Spoon 1 tablespoon pork onto center of each biscuit. Gather edges around filling and press to seal.

2. Generously butter 2-quart baking dish that fits inside **CROCK-POT**® slow cooker. Arrange filled biscuits in single layer, overlapping slightly if necessary. Cover dish with buttered foil, butter side down.

3. Place small rack in **CROCK-POT**® slow cooker or prop up baking dish with a few equal-size potatoes. Add 1 inch hot water (water should not come to top of rack). Place baking dish on rack. Cover; cook on HIGH 2 hours.

4. Meanwhile, prepare Dipping Sauce. Garnish pork buns with green onions, if desired. Serve with dipping sauce.

Makes 8 servings

Dipping Sauce: Stir together 2 tablespoons rice vinegar, 2 tablespoons reduced-sodium soy sauce, 4 teaspoons sugar and 1 teaspoon toasted sesame oil in a small bowl until sugar dissolves. Sprinkle with 1 tablespoon minced green onion (green part only) just before serving.

PREP TIME: 30 minutes
COOK TIME: 2 hours (HIGH)

Rosemary Pork with Red Wine Risotto

1 boneless pork loin (about 3 pounds)

1 teaspoon salt

1 teaspoon black pepper

2 tablespoons olive oil

6 sprigs fresh rosemary, divided

2 cups chicken broth, divided

2 tablespoons butter, divided

3 cloves garlic, minced

½ cup minced onion

1 cup Arborio rice

1 cup fruity red wine

¾ cup grated Parmesan cheese

1. Season pork with salt and pepper. Heat oil in large skillet over medium-high heat until hot. Add 3 sprigs of rosemary and place pork roast on top. Brown pork roast on all sides, about 5 to 7 minutes. Transfer roast and rosemary to **CROCK-POT®** slow cooker.

2. Add ¼ cup broth to skillet. Cook and stir, loosening browned bits. Add 1 tablespoon butter, garlic and onion. Cook and stir until onion is translucent.

3. Add rice to skillet. Cook and stir until rice just begins to brown, about 2 minutes. Stir in wine and remaining 1¾ cups broth. Pour mixture around roast. Cover; cook on HIGH 3 to 4 hours, stirring occasionally, until roast reaches 160°F on thermometer inserted into center.

4. Remove and discard rosemary. Transfer roast to serving platter. Let stand 10 minutes before slicing.

5. Stir remaining 1 tablespoon butter and Parmesan cheese into rice. Serve risotto with roast and garnish with remaining rosemary.

Makes 4 to 6 servings

PREP TIME: 15 minutes
COOK TIME: 3 to 4 hours (HIGH)

Thai Chicken

2½ pounds chicken pieces
1 cup hot salsa
¼ cup peanut butter
2 tablespoons lime juice
1 tablespoon soy sauce

1 teaspoon minced fresh ginger
Hot cooked rice (optional)
½ cup peanuts, chopped
2 tablespoons chopped fresh cilantro

1. Place chicken in **CROCK-POT**® slow cooker. Mix together salsa, peanut butter, lime juice, soy sauce and ginger; pour over chicken.

2. Cover; cook on LOW 8 to 9 hours or on HIGH 3 to 4 hours or until done.

3. Serve over rice, if desired, topped with sauce, peanuts and cilantro.

Makes 6 servings

PREP TIME: 10 to 15 minutes
COOK TIME : 8 to 9 hours (LOW) or 3 to 4 hours (HIGH)

Turkey Breast with Barley-Cranberry Stuffing

- **2** cups reduced-sodium chicken broth
- **1** cup uncooked quick-cooking barley
- **½** cup chopped onion
- **½** cup dried cranberries
- **2** tablespoons slivered almonds, toasted*
- **½** teaspoon rubbed sage
- **½** teaspoon garlic-pepper seasoning
- **1** fresh or thawed frozen bone-in turkey breast half (about 2 pounds), skinned
- **⅓** cup finely chopped fresh parsley

*To toast almonds, spread in single layer on baking sheet. Bake in preheated 350°F oven 8 to 10 minutes or until golden brown, stirring frequently.

1. Combine broth, barley, onion, cranberries, almonds, sage and garlic-pepper seasoning in **CROCK-POT**® slow cooker.

2. Coat large nonstick skillet with cooking spray. Heat over medium heat until hot. Brown turkey breast on all sides; add to **CROCK-POT**® slow cooker. Cover; cook on LOW 4 to 6 hours.

3. Transfer turkey to cutting board; cover with foil to keep warm. Let stand 10 to 15 minutes before carving. Stir parsley into sauce mixture in **CROCK-POT**® slow cooker. Serve over sliced turkey and stuffing.

Makes 6 servings

Tip: Browning poultry before cooking it in the **CROCK-POT**® slow cooker isn't necessary but helps to enhance the flavor and adds an oven-roasted appearance to the finished dish.

PREP TIME: 15 minutes
COOK TIME: 4 to 6 hours (LOW)

Burgundy and Wild Cremini Mushroom Pilaf

2 tablespoons vegetable oil

2 cups converted long-grain white rice

1 medium onion, chopped

1 cup sliced wild cremini mushrooms

1 small zucchini, thinly sliced

3½ cups beef or vegetable broth

½ cup burgundy or other red wine

½ teaspoon salt

¼ teaspoon black pepper

4 tablespoons (½ stick) butter, melted

1. Heat oil in skillet over medium heat until hot. Add rice, onion, mushrooms and zucchini. Cook and stir 4 to 5 minutes until rice is slightly browned and onion is soft. Transfer to **CROCK-POT**® slow cooker.

2. Add broth, burgundy, salt and pepper. Drizzle melted butter over all. Stir once. Cover; cook on LOW 6 to 8 hours.

Makes 6 servings

PREP TIME: 15 minutes
COOK TIME: 6 to 8 hours (LOW)

Creamy Red Pepper Polenta

4 tablespoons (½ stick) butter, melted

¼ teaspoon paprika, plus additional for garnish

⅛ teaspoon ground red pepper

⅛ teaspoon ground cumin

6 cups boiling water

2 cups yellow cornmeal

1 small red bell pepper, cored, seeded and finely chopped

2 teaspoons salt

Combine butter, paprika, red pepper and cumin in **CROCK-POT**® slow cooker. Add hot water, cornmeal, red bell pepper and salt. Stir well to combine. Cover; cook on LOW 3 to 4 hours or on HIGH 1 to 2 hours, stirring occasionally. Garnish with additional paprika, if desired.

Makes 4 to 6 servings

PREP TIME: 10 minutes
COOK TIME: 3 to 4 hours (LOW) or 1 to 2 hours (HIGH)

Spicy Citrus Pork with Pineapple Salsa

1 tablespoon ground cumin

½ teaspoon salt

1 teaspoon coarsely ground black pepper

3 pounds center-cut pork loin, rinsed and patted dry

2 tablespoons vegetable oil

4 cans (8 ounces each) pineapple tidbits* in own juice, drained, ½ cup juice reserved

4 tablespoons lemon juice, divided

2 teaspoons grated lemon peel

1 cup finely chopped orange or red bell pepper

4 tablespoons finely chopped red onion

2 tablespoons chopped fresh cilantro or mint

1 teaspoon grated fresh ginger (optional)

¼ teaspoon red pepper flakes (optional)

*If tidbits are unavailable, purchase pineapple chunks and coarsely chop.

1. Coat **CROCK-POT**® slow cooker with nonstick cooking spray. Combine cumin, salt and pepper in small bowl. Rub evenly onto pork. Heat oil in medium skillet over medium-high heat until hot. Sear pork loin on all sides, turning as it browns, 1 to 2 minutes per side. Transfer to **CROCK-POT**® slow cooker.

2. Spoon 4 tablespoons of reserved pineapple juice and 2 tablespoons lemon juice over pork. Cover; cook on LOW 2 to 2¼ hours or on HIGH 1 hour and 10 minutes, or until meat is tender.

3. Meanwhile, combine all remaining ingredients including ginger, if desired, and pepper flakes, if desired, in medium bowl. Toss to blend well; set aside.

4. Let pork stand 10 minutes before slicing. Arrange pork slices on serving platter. To serve, pour sauce evenly over slices. Serve salsa on side.

Makes 12 servings

PREP TIME: 20 minutes
COOK TIME: 2 to 2¼ hours (LOW) or 1 hour (HIGH)

Ham with Fruited Bourbon Sauce

1 **bone-in ham, butt portion (about 6 pounds)**	¼ **teaspoon red pepper flakes**
½ **cup apple juice**	⅓ **cup dried cherries**
¾ **cup packed dark brown sugar**	¼ **cup cornstarch**
½ **cup raisins**	¼ **cup bourbon, rum or apple juice**
1 **teaspoon ground cinnamon**	

1. Coat **CROCK-POT**® slow cooker with nonstick cooking spray. Add ham, cut-side up. Combine apple juice, brown sugar, raisins, cinnamon and red pepper flakes in small bowl; stir well. Pour mixture evenly over ham. Cover; cook on LOW 9 to 10 hours or on HIGH 4½ to 5 hours. Add cherries 30 minutes before end of cooking time.

2. Transfer ham to cutting board. Let stand 15 minutes before slicing.

3. Pour cooking liquid into large measuring cup and let stand 5 minutes. Skim and discard excess fat. Return cooking liquid to **CROCK-POT**® slow cooker.

4. Turn **CROCK-POT**® slow cooker to HIGH. Whisk cornstarch and bourbon in small bowl until cornstarch is dissolved. Stir into cooking liquid. Cover; cook on HIGH 15 to 20 minutes longer or until thickened. Serve sauce over sliced ham.

Makes 10 to 12 servings

Tip: For easier cleanup of the **CROCK-POT**® slow cooker stoneware, spray the inside with nonstick cooking spray before adding ingredients.

PREP TIME: 5 minutes
COOK TIME: 9 to 10 hours (LOW) or 4½ to 5 hours (HIGH) plus 15 minutes (HIGH)

Chicken Cordon Bleu

¼ cup all-purpose flour

1 teaspoon paprika

½ teaspoon salt

¼ teaspoon black pepper

4 boneless chicken breasts, lightly pounded*

4 slices ham

4 slices Swiss cheese

2 tablespoons olive oil

½ cup white cooking wine

½ cup chicken broth

½ cup half-and-half

2 tablespoons cornstarch

*Place chicken between 2 pieces of plastic food wrap and flatten with back of skillet.

1. Combine flour, paprika, salt and pepper in resealable plastic food storage bag and shake well; set aside.

2. Place flattened chicken on cutting board, skin side down. Place 1 slice ham and 1 slice cheese on each piece. Fold chicken up to enclose filling and secure with toothpick. Place in bag with seasoned flour and shake gently to coat.

3. Heat oil in large skillet over medium-high heat until hot. Add chicken, skin side down. Brown on all sides. Transfer to **CROCK-POT**® slow cooker.

4. Remove skillet from heat and add wine. Cook and stir to loosen browned bits. Pour into **CROCK-POT**® slow cooker. Add broth. Cover; cook on LOW 2 hours.

5. Remove chicken with slotted spoon. Cover with aluminum foil to keep warm. Mix together half-and-half and cornstarch. Add to cooking liquid. Cover, cook on LOW 15 minutes longer or until sauce has thickened. To serve, remove toothpicks, place chicken on plates and spoon sauce around chicken. Serve extra sauce on side.

Makes 4 servings

PREP TIME: 20 minutes
COOK TIME: 2½ hours (LOW)

Indian-Style Apricot Chicken

6 skinless chicken thighs, rinsed and patted dry

¼ teaspoon salt

¼ teaspoon black pepper

1 tablespoon vegetable oil

1 large onion, chopped

2 cloves garlic, minced

2 tablespoons grated fresh ginger

½ teaspoon ground cinnamon

⅛ teaspoon ground allspice

1 can (14½ ounces) diced tomatoes, undrained

1 cup chicken broth

1 package (8 ounces) dried apricots

1 pinch saffron threads (optional)

Hot basmati rice

2 tablespoons chopped fresh parsley (optional)

1. Coat **CROCK-POT**® slow cooker with nonstick cooking spray. Season chicken with salt and pepper. Heat oil in large skillet over medium-high heat until hot. Brown chicken on all sides. Transfer to prepared **CROCK-POT**® slow cooker.

2. Add onion to skillet. Cook and stir 3 to 5 minutes or until translucent. Stir in garlic, ginger, cinnamon and allspice. Cook and stir 15 to 30 seconds longer or until mixture is fragrant. Add tomatoes with juice and broth. Cook 2 to 3 minutes or until mixture is heated through. Pour into **CROCK-POT**® slow cooker.

3. Add apricots and saffron, if desired. Cover; cook on LOW 5 to 6 hours or on HIGH 3 to 4 hours or until chicken is tender. Add salt and pepper, if desired. Serve with basmati rice and garnish with chopped parsley, if desired.

Makes 4 to 6 servings

PREP TIME: 15 minutes
COOK TIME: 5 to 6 hours (LOW) or 3 to 4 hours (HIGH)

Cran-Orange-Acorn Squash

3 small acorn or carnival squash
5 tablespoons instant brown rice
3 tablespoons minced onion
3 tablespoons diced celery
3 tablespoons dried cranberries

Pinch ground or dried sage
1 teaspoon butter, cut into bits
3 tablespoons orange juice
½ cup warm water

1. Slice off tops of squash and enough of bottoms so squash will sit upright. Scoop out seeds and discard; set squash aside.

2. Combine rice, onion, celery, cranberries and sage in small bowl. Stuff each squash with rice mixture; dot with butter. Pour 1 tablespoon orange juice into each squash over stuffing. Stand squash in **CROCK-POT**® slow cooker. Pour water into bottom of slow cooker.

3. Cover; cook on LOW 2½ hours or until squash are tender.

Makes 6 servings

PREP TIME: 20 minutes
COOK TIME: 2½ hours (LOW)

Caribbean Shrimp with Rice

1 package (12 ounces) frozen shrimp, thawed
½ cup fat-free, reduced-sodium chicken broth
1 clove garlic, minced
1 teaspoon chili powder
½ teaspoon salt
½ teaspoon dried oregano
1 cup frozen peas, thawed
½ cup diced tomatoes
2 cups cooked long-grain white rice

1. Combine shrimp, broth, garlic, chili powder, salt and oregano in **CROCK-POT®** slow cooker. Cover; cook on LOW 2 hours.

2. Add peas and tomatoes. Cover; cook on LOW 5 minutes. Stir in rice. Cover; cook on LOW 5 minutes longer, or until rice is heated through.

Makes 4 servings

PREP TIME: 10 minutes
COOK TIME: 2 hours 10 minutes (LOW)

Asian Pork Ribs with Spicy Noodles

1 can (14 ounces) beef broth

½ cup water

¼ cup rice wine vinegar

1 ounce (2-inch piece) fresh ginger, peeled and grated

1 cup (about 1 ounce) dried sliced shiitake mushrooms

¼ teaspoon red pepper flakes

1 tablespoon Chinese five-spice powder

1 teaspoon ground ginger

1 teaspoon chili powder

1 tablespoon dark sesame oil

2 full racks pork back ribs (about 4 pounds total)

¾ cup hoisin sauce, divided

1 pound (16 ounces) thin spaghetti, cooked according to package directions

¼ cup thinly sliced green onions

¼ cup chopped fresh cilantro

1. Stir together beef broth, water, rice wine vinegar, grated ginger, shiitake mushrooms and red pepper flakes in a **CROCK-POT**® slow cooker.

2. Stir together five-spice powder, ground ginger, chili powder and sesame oil to form a paste. Blot ribs dry with paper towels. Rub both sides with spice paste and brush with half of hoisin sauce.

3. Place ribs in **CROCK-POT**® slow cooker with prepared cooking liquid (do not stir). Cover and cook on LOW 8 to 10 hours or on HIGH 5 to 6 hours or until meat is tender when pierced with a fork. Remove ribs to platter and brush lightly with remaining hoisin sauce. Keep warm until serving. Meanwhile, skim off any fat from cooking liquid.

4. Place warm spaghetti in shallow bowl. Ladle some hot broth over spaghetti and sprinkle with green onions and cilantro. Slice ribs and serve over pasta.

Makes 4 servings

PREP TIME: 20 minutes
COOK TIME: 8 to 10 hours (LOW) 5 to 6 hours (HIGH)

Greek Chicken and Orzo

2 medium green bell peppers,
   cut into thin strips

1 cup chopped onion

2 teaspoons extra-virgin olive oil

8 chicken thighs, rinsed and
   patted dry

1 tablespoon dried oregano

½ teaspoon dried rosemary

½ teaspoon garlic powder

¾ teaspoon salt, divided

⅜ teaspoon black pepper,
   divided

8 ounces uncooked orzo pasta

Juice and grated peel of
   1 medium lemon

½ cup water

2 ounces crumbled feta cheese
   (optional)

Chopped fresh parsley
   (optional)

1. Coat **CROCK-POT**® slow cooker with nonstick cooking spray. Add bell peppers and onion.

2. Heat oil in large skillet over medium-high heat until hot. Brown chicken on both sides. Transfer to **CROCK-POT**® slow cooker, overlapping slightly if necessary. Sprinkle chicken with oregano, rosemary, garlic powder, ¼ teaspoon salt and ⅛ teaspoon black pepper. Cover; cook on LOW 5 to 6 hours or on HIGH 3 to 4 hours, or until chicken is tender.

3. Transfer chicken to separate plate. Turn **CROCK-POT**® slow cooker to HIGH. Stir orzo, lemon juice, lemon peel, water, remaining ½ teaspoon salt and ¼ teaspoon black pepper into **CROCK-POT**® slow cooker. Top with chicken. Cover; cook 30 minutes or until pasta is done. Garnish with feta cheese and parsley, if desired.

Makes 4 servings

PREP TIME: 5 minutes
COOK TIME: 5½ to 6½ hours (LOW) or 3½ to 4½ hours (HIGH)

Pesto Rice and Beans

1 can (15 ounces) Great Northern beans, rinsed and drained

1 can (14 ounces) chicken broth

¾ cup uncooked converted long-grain rice

1½ cups frozen cut green beans, thawed and drained

½ cup prepared pesto

Grated Parmesan cheese (optional)

1. Combine beans, broth and rice in **CROCK-POT**® slow cooker. Cover; cook on LOW 2 hours.

2. Stir in green beans. Cover; cook 1 hour or until rice and beans are tender.

3. Turn off **CROCK-POT**® slow cooker and transfer stoneware to heatproof surface. Stir in pesto and Parmesan cheese, if desired. Let stand, covered, 5 minutes or until cheese is melted. Serve immediately.

Makes 8 servings

Tip: Choose converted long-grain rice (or Arborio rice when suggested) or wild rice for best results. Long, slow cooking can turn other types of rice into mush; if you prefer to use another type of rice instead of converted rice, cook it on the stove-top and add it to the **CROCK-POT**® slow cooker during the last 15 minutes of cooking.

PREP TIME: 10 minutes
COOK TIME: 3 hours (LOW)

Chicken Croustade

2 tablespoons canola oil

1½ pounds boneless, skinless chicken breasts, cut into ¼-inch pieces

Salt and black pepper

1 shallot, minced

¼ cup white wine

1 large portobello mushroom cap

1 tablespoon chopped fresh thyme

¼ teaspoon sweet paprika

¼ teaspoon ground cumin

¼ cup chicken broth

1 package puff pastry shells

1 egg yolk

2 tablespoons cream

3 tablespoons freshly grated Parmesan cheese

Minced and whole chives (optional)

1. Heat oil in large skillet over medium-high heat. Season chicken with salt and pepper and cook until brown on both sides. Transfer to **CROCK-POT**® slow cooker. Return skillet to heat and add shallot. Cook until shallot softens. Stir in white wine, scraping up any brown bits with wooden spoon. Continue to cook until reduced to 2 tablespoons, then pour over chicken.

2. Scrape gills from mushroom cap and discard. Chop mushroom into ¼-inch pieces. Stir chopped mushroom, thyme, paprika, cumin and broth into **CROCK-POT**® slow cooker with chicken. Cover and cook on LOW 3 hours.

3. Two hours after starting to cook chicken, cook puff pastry shells according to package directions and cool completely.

4. Twenty minutes before end of cooking time, beat egg yolk and cream together. Stir 1 tablespoon hot cooking liquid into egg mixture. Beat until well combined, then stir into remaining cooking liquid. Continue cooking on LOW, uncovered, 20 minutes. Stir in Parmesan cheese. Divide chicken filling among puff pastry shells. Serve garnished with chives, if desired.

Makes 6 to 8 servings

PREP TIME: 45 minutes
COOK TIME: 3 hours (LOW)

Coq au Vin

2 cups frozen pearl onions, thawed

4 slices thick-cut bacon, crisp-cooked and crumbled

1 cup sliced button mushrooms

1 clove garlic, minced

1 teaspoon dried thyme

⅛ teaspoon black pepper

6 boneless, skinless chicken breasts (about 2 pounds)

½ cup dry red wine

¾ cup reduced-sodium chicken broth

¼ cup tomato paste

3 tablespoons all-purpose flour

Hot cooked egg noodles (optional)

1. Layer onions, bacon, mushrooms, garlic, thyme, pepper, chicken, wine and broth in **CROCK-POT**® slow cooker.

2. Cover; cook on LOW 6 to 8 hours.

3. Remove chicken and vegetables; cover and keep warm. Ladle ½ cup cooking liquid into small bowl; cool slightly. Mix reserved liquid, tomato paste and flour until smooth; stir into **CROCK-POT**® slow cooker. Cook; uncovered, on HIGH 15 minutes or until thickened. Serve over hot noodles, if desired.

Makes 6 servings

Tip: Coq au Vin is a classic French dish that is made with bone-in chicken, salt pork or bacon, brandy, red wine and herbs. The dish originated when farmers needed a way to cook old chickens that could no longer breed. A slow, moist cooking method was needed to tenderize the tough old birds.

PREP TIME: 15 minutes
COOK TIME: 6 to 8 hours (LOW) plus 15 minutes (HIGH)

Dijon Chicken Thighs with Artichoke Sauce

½ cup Dijon mustard

2 tablespoons chopped garlic

½ teaspoon dried tarragon

2½ pounds skinless chicken thighs (about 8)

1 cup chopped onion

1 cup sliced mushrooms

1 jar (12 ounces) quartered marinated artichoke hearts, undrained

¼ cup chopped fresh parsley

1. Combine mustard, garlic and tarragon in large bowl. Add chicken thighs and toss to coat. Transfer to **CROCK-POT**® slow cooker.

2. Add onion, mushrooms and artichokes with liquid. Cover; cook on LOW 6 to 8 hours or on HIGH 4 hours or until chicken is tender. Stir in parsley just before serving.

Makes 8 servings

Note: To skin chicken easily, grasp skin with paper towel and pull away. Repeat with fresh paper towel for each piece of chicken, discarding skins and towels.

Serving Suggestion: Serve with hot fettuccine that has been tossed with butter and chopped parsley.

PREP TIME: 10 minutes
COOK TIME: 6 to 8 hours (LOW) or 4 hours (HIGH)

Moroccan-Style Lamb Shoulder Chops with Couscous

4 lamb blade chops (about 2½ pounds)

Salt and black pepper, to taste

1 tablespoon olive oil

1 onion, chopped

1 clove garlic, minced

1 teaspoon grated fresh ginger

¼ teaspoon ground cinnamon

½ teaspoon ground turmeric

½ teaspoon salt

¼ teaspoon black pepper

1 bay leaf

1 can (14½ ounces) diced tomatoes, undrained

1 cup canned chickpeas, rinsed and drained

½ cup water

2 tablespoons lemon juice

Hot cooked couscous

Lemon wedges (optional)

1. Coat **CROCK-POT**® slow cooker with nonstick cooking spray. Season lamb chops with salt and pepper. Heat oil in large skillet over medium-high heat until hot. Add lamb chops and brown on all sides. Transfer to **CROCK-POT**® slow cooker.

2. Add onion to skillet. Cook and stir 2 to 3 minutes or until translucent. Add garlic, ginger, cinnamon, turmeric, salt, pepper and bay leaf. Cook and stir 30 seconds longer. Stir in tomatoes with juice, chickpeas, water and lemon juice. Simmer 2 minutes. Pour mixture over lamb. Cover; cook on HIGH 3½ to 4 hours or until lamb is tender.

3. Add salt and pepper, if desired. Serve lamb chops over couscous with sauce and vegetables. Serve with lemon wedges, if desired.

Makes 4 servings

Tip: Add fresh lemon juice just before serving to enhance flavors.

PREP TIME: 15 minutes
COOK TIME: 3½ to 4 hours (HIGH)

Curry Chicken with Peaches and Raisins

2 peaches, peeled and sliced into ¼-inch slices, reserving 8 slices for garnish

Lemon juice

4 skinless chicken thighs (or 2 boneless, skinless chicken breasts)

Salt and black pepper, to taste

1 tablespoon olive oil

⅓ cup raisins, chopped, or ⅓ cup currants, whole

1 shallot, thinly sliced

1 tablespoon grated fresh ginger

2 cloves garlic, crushed

½ teaspoon curry powder

1 teaspoon ground cumin

½ teaspoon whole cloves

¼ cup chicken stock

1 tablespoon cider vinegar

¼ teaspoon ground red pepper (optional)

1 teaspoon cornstarch (optional)

Fresh cilantro leaves (optional)

Hot cooked rice (optional)

1. Toss 8 slices of peaches with lemon juice to coat and refrigerate. Rinse, dry and season chicken with salt and black pepper.

2. Heat olive oil in skillet until hot. Add chicken and lightly brown, about 3 minutes per side. Transfer to **CROCK-POT**® slow cooker. Top with remaining peaches, raisins and shallot.

3. Whisk together ginger, garlic, curry, cumin, cloves, stock, vinegar and ground red pepper, if desired. Pour mixture over chicken. Cover; cook on LOW 5 hours or on HIGH 3 to 3½ hours.

4. Transfer chicken to serving dish. Stir cornstarch into sauce to thicken, if desired. Spoon peaches, raisins and sauce over chicken. Top with reserved peaches and cilantro, if desired. Serve over rice, if desired.

Makes 2 servings

PREP TIME: 15 minutes
COOK TIME: 5 hours (LOW) or 3 to 3½ hours (HIGH)

Chipotle Cornish Hens

3 small carrots, cut into ½-inch rounds

3 stalks celery, cut into ½-inch pieces

1 onion, chopped

1 can (7 ounces) chipotle peppers in adobo sauce, divided

2 cups prepared cornbread stuffing

4 Cornish hens (about 1½ pounds each)

Salt and black pepper, to taste

Fresh parsley, chopped (optional)

1. Coat **CROCK-POT**® slow cooker with nonstick cooking spray. Add carrots, celery and onion.

2. Pour canned chipotles into small bowl. Finely chop 1 chipotle pepper. Remove remaining peppers from adobo sauce and reserve for another use. Mix ½ of chopped chipotle pepper into prepared stuffing. Add remaining ½ of chopped chipotle pepper to adobo sauce.*

3. Rinse and dry hens, removing giblets, if any. Season with salt and black pepper inside and out. Fill each hen with about ½ cup stuffing. Rub adobo sauce onto hens. Place in **CROCK-POT**® slow cooker, arranging hens neck down and legs up. Cover; cook on HIGH 3½ to 4½ hours or until hens are cooked through and tender.

4. Transfer hens to serving platter. Remove vegetables with slotted spoon and arrange around hens. Garnish with parsley, if desired. Spoon cooking juices over hens and vegetables, if desired.

Makes 4 servings

*For spicier flavor, use 1 chipotle pepper in stuffing and 1 chipotle pepper in sauce.

PREP TIME: 5 minutes
COOK TIME: 3½ to 4½ hours (HIGH)

Family
Dinners

Nice 'N' Easy Italian Chicken

4 boneless, skinless chicken breasts (about 1 pound)

8 ounces mushrooms, sliced

1 medium green bell pepper, chopped

1 medium zucchini, diced

1 medium onion, chopped

1 jar (26 ounces) pasta sauce

Hot cooked linguini or spaghetti

Combine all ingredients except pasta in **CROCK-POT**® slow cooker. Cover; cook on LOW 6 to 8 hours or until chicken is tender. Serve over linguini.

Makes 4 servings

PREP TIME: 10 minutes
COOK TIME: 6 to 8 hours (LOW)

Philly Cheese Steaks

2 pounds round steak, sliced

2 tablespoons butter or margarine, melted

4 onions, sliced

2 green bell peppers, sliced

1 tablespoon garlic-pepper blend

Salt, to taste

½ cup water

2 teaspoons beef bouillon granules

8 crusty Italian or French rolls*

8 slices Cheddar cheese, cut in half

*Toast rolls under broiler or on griddle, if desired.

1. Combine steak, butter, onions, green pepper, garlic-pepper blend and salt in **CROCK-POT**® slow cooker; stir to mix.

2. Whisk together water and bouillon in small bowl; pour into **CROCK-POT**® slow cooker. Cover; cook on LOW 6 to 8 hours.

3. Remove meat, onions and bell pepper from **CROCK-POT**® slow cooker and pile on rolls. Top with cheese and place under broiler until cheese is melted.

Makes 8 servings

PREP TIME: 10 to 15 minutes
COOK TIME: 6 to 8 hours (LOW)

Campfired-Up Sloppy Joes

1½ pounds lean ground beef

½ cup chopped sweet onion

1 medium red bell pepper, cored, seeded and chopped

1 large clove garlic, crushed

½ cup ketchup

½ cup barbecue sauce

2 tablespoons cider vinegar

1 tablespoon Worcestershire sauce

1 tablespoon packed brown sugar

1 teaspoon chili powder

1 can (8 ounces) baked beans

6 kaiser rolls, split and warmed

Shredded sharp Cheddar cheese (optional)

1. Brown ground beef, onion, bell pepper and garlic 6 to 8 minutes in large skillet over medium-high heat, stirring to break up meat. Drain and discard excess fat. Transfer beef mixture to **CROCK-POT**® slow cooker.

2. Combine ketchup, barbecue sauce, vinegar, Worcestershire sauce, brown sugar and chili powder in small bowl. Transfer to **CROCK-POT**® slow cooker.

3. Add baked beans. Stir well to combine. Cover; cook on HIGH 3 hours.

4. To serve, fill split rolls with ½ cup sloppy joe mixture. Sprinkle with Cheddar cheese, if desired, before topping sandwich with roll lid.

Makes 4 to 6 servings

Serving Suggestion: Serve with a side of coleslaw.

PREP TIME: 20 minutes
COOK TIME: 3 hours (HIGH)

Chicken and Spicy Black Bean Tacos

1 can (15 ounces) black beans, rinsed and drained

1 can (10 ounces) tomatoes with mild green chiles, drained

1½ teaspoons chili powder

¾ teaspoon ground cumin

1 tablespoon plus 1 teaspoon extra-virgin olive oil, divided

12 ounces boneless, skinless chicken breasts, rinsed and patted dry

12 crisp corn taco shells

Optional toppings: shredded lettuce, diced tomatoes, shredded cheese, sour cream, ripe olives

1. Coat **CROCK-POT**® slow cooker with nonstick cooking spray. Add beans and tomatoes with chiles. Blend chili powder and cumin with 1 teaspoon oil and rub onto chicken breasts. Place chicken in **CROCK-POT**® slow cooker. Cover; cook on HIGH 1¾ hours.

2. Remove chicken and slice. Transfer bean mixture to bowl using slotted spoon. Stir in 1 tablespoon oil.

3. To serve, warm taco shells according to package directions. Fill with equal amounts of bean mixture and chicken. Top as desired.

Makes 4 servings

PREP TIME: 10 minutes
COOK TIME: 1¾ hours (HIGH)

Asian Beef with Broccoli

1½ pounds boneless chuck steak, about 1½ inches thick, sliced into thin strips*

1 can (10½ ounces) condensed beef consommé, undiluted

½ cup oyster sauce

2 tablespoons cornstarch

1 bag (16 ounces) fresh broccoli florets

Hot cooked rice

Sesame seeds (optional)

*To make slicing steak easier, place in freezer for 30 minutes to firm up.

1. Place beef in **CROCK-POT**® slow cooker. Pour consommé and oyster sauce over beef. Cover; cook on HIGH 3 hours.

2. Combine cornstarch and 2 tablespoons cooking liquid in small bowl. Stir well to combine. Stir into **CROCK-POT**® slow cooker. Cover; cook on HIGH 15 minutes longer or until thickened.

3. Poke holes in broccoli bag with fork. Microwave on HIGH (100% power) 3 minutes. Empty bag into **CROCK-POT**® slow cooker. Gently toss beef and broccoli together. Serve over cooked rice. Garnish with sesame seeds, if desired.

Makes 4 to 6 servings

PREP TIME: 15 minutes
COOK TIME: 3¼ hours (HIGH)

Lemon Pork Chops

1 tablespoon vegetable oil

4 boneless pork chops

3 cans (8 ounces each) tomato sauce

1 large onion, quartered and sliced (optional)

1 large green bell pepper, cut into strips

1 tablespoon lemon-pepper seasoning

1 tablespoon Worcestershire sauce

1 large lemon, quartered
  Lemon wedges (optional)

1. Heat oil in large skillet over medium-low heat until hot. Brown pork chops on both sides. Drain excess fat and discard. Transfer to **CROCK-POT**® slow cooker.

2. Combine tomato sauce, onion, if desired, bell pepper, lemon-pepper seasoning and Worcestershire sauce. Add to **CROCK-POT**® slow cooker.

3. Squeeze juice from lemon quarters over mixture; drop squeezed lemons into **CROCK-POT**® slow cooker. Cover; cook on LOW 6 to 8 hours or until pork is tender. Remove squeezed lemons before serving. Garnish with additional lemon wedges, if desired.

Makes 4 servings

Tip: Browning pork before adding it to the **CROCK-POT**® slow cooker helps reduce the fat. Just remember to drain off the fat in the skillet before transferring the pork to the **CROCK-POT**® slow cooker.

PREP TIME: 15 to 20 minutes
COOK TIME: 6 to 8 hours (LOW)

Fall-Apart Pork Roast with Mole

⅔ **cup whole almonds**

⅔ **cup raisins**

3 **tablespoons vegetable oil, divided**

½ **cup chopped onion**

4 **cloves garlic, chopped**

2¾ **pounds lean boneless pork shoulder roast, well trimmed**

1 **can (14½ ounces) diced fire-roasted tomatoes or diced tomatoes, undrained**

1 **cup cubed bread, any variety**

½ **cup chicken broth**

2 **ounces Mexican chocolate, chopped**

2 **tablespoons chipotle peppers in adobo sauce, chopped**

1 **teaspoon salt**

Fresh cilantro, coarsely chopped (optional)

1. Heat large skillet over medium-high heat until hot. Add almonds and toast 3 to 4 minutes, stirring frequently, until fragrant. Add raisins. Cook 1 to 2 minutes longer, stirring constantly, until raisins plump. Place half of mixture in large mixing bowl. Reserve remaining half for garnish. In same skillet, heat 1 tablespoon oil. Add onion and garlic. Cook and stir 2 to 3 minutes until softened. Add to almond mixture; set aside.

2. Heat remaining oil in same skillet. Add pork roast and brown on all sides, about 5 to 7 minutes per side. Transfer to **CROCK-POT**® slow cooker.

3. Process almond mixture, tomatoes with juice, bread, broth, chocolate and chipotle peppers in blender until smooth. Pour purée over pork roast. Cover; cook on LOW 7 to 8 hours or on HIGH 3 to 4 hours or until pork is done.

4. Remove pork roast from **CROCK-POT**® slow cooker. Whisk sauce until smooth before spooning over pork roast. Garnish with reserved almond mixture and chopped cilantro, if desired.

Makes 6 servings

PREP TIME: 30 minutes
COOK TIME: 7 to 8 hours (LOW) or 3 to 4 hours (HIGH)

Chicken and Ham with Biscuits

2 cans (10¾ ounces each) cream of mushroom soup

2 cups diced ham

2 cups diced boneless chicken

1 package (12 ounces) frozen peas and onions

1 package (8 ounces) frozen corn

½ cup chopped celery

¼ teaspoon dried marjoram

¼ teaspoon dried thyme

2 tablespoons cornstarch

2 teaspoons water

1 to 2 cans refrigerated buttermilk biscuits

4 tablespoons (½ stick) butter, melted

1. Combine soup, ham, chicken, frozen vegetables, celery, marjoram and thyme in **CROCK-POT**® slow cooker. Cover; cook on LOW 4 to 5 hours or on HIGH 1 to 3 hours.

2. Mix cornstarch and water together in bowl. Stir into **CROCK-POT**® slow cooker. Cook 10 to 15 minutes longer or until mixture has thickened.

3. Meanwhile, place biscuits on baking sheet and brush with butter. Bake according to package directions until biscuits are golden brown.

4. To serve, ladle stew into bowls and top with warm biscuit.

Makes 8 to 10 servings

PREP TIME: 10 minutes
COOK TIME: 4¼ to 5¼ hours (LOW) or 1¼ to 3¼ hours (HIGH)

Mama's Best Baked Beans

1 bag (1 pound) dried Great Northern beans

1 package (1 pound) bacon

5 hot dogs, cut into ½-inch pieces

1 cup chopped onion

1 bottle (24 ounces) ketchup

2 cups packed dark brown sugar

1. Soak and cook beans according to package directions. Drain and refrigerate until ready to use.

2. Cook bacon in large skillet over medium-high heat until crisp. Transfer to paper towels to drain. Cool, then crumble bacon; set aside. Discard all but 3 tablespoons bacon fat from skillet. Add hot dogs and onion. Cook and stir over medium heat until onion is tender.

3. Combine cooked beans, bacon, hot dog mixture, ketchup and brown sugar in **CROCK-POT**® slow cooker. Cover; cook on LOW 2 to 4 hours.

Makes 4 to 6 servings

PREP TIME: 30 minutes
COOK TIME: 2 to 4 hours (LOW)

Deluxe Potato Casserole

1 can (10¾ ounces) condensed
    cream of chicken soup,
    undiluted

1 container (8 ounces) sour
    cream

¼ cup chopped onion

¼ cup (½ stick) plus
    3 tablespoons melted butter,
    divided

1 teaspoon salt

2 pounds red potatoes, peeled
    and diced

2 cups (8 ounces) shredded
    Cheddar cheese

1½ to 2 cups stuffing mix

1. Combine soup, sour cream, onion, ¼ cup butter and salt in small bowl.

2. Combine potatoes and cheese in **CROCK-POT®** slow cooker. Pour soup mixture over potato mixture; mix well. Sprinkle stuffing mix over potato mixture; drizzle with remaining 3 tablespoons butter. Cover; cook on LOW 8 to 10 hours or on HIGH 5 to 6 hours, or until potatoes are tender.

Makes 8 to 10 servings

PREP TIME: 10 minutes
COOK TIME: 8 to 10 hours (LOW) or 5 to 6 hours (HIGH)

Easy Beef Stroganoff

3 cans (10¾ ounces each) condensed cream of mushroom soup, undiluted

1 cup sour cream

½ cup water

1 package (1 ounce) dry onion soup mix

2 pounds beef stew meat, cut into 1-inch pieces

Combine soup, sour cream, water and soup mix in **CROCK-POT®** slow cooker. Add beef; stir until well coated. Cover; cook on LOW 6 hours or on HIGH 3 hours.

Makes 4 to 6 servings

PREP TIME: 5 minutes
COOK TIME: 6 hours (LOW) or 3 hours (HIGH)

Cuban Pork Sandwiches

1 pork loin roast (about 2 pounds)	8 crusty bread rolls, split in half (6 inches each)
½ cup orange juice	2 tablespoons yellow mustard
2 tablespoons lime juice	8 slices Swiss cheese
1 tablespoon minced garlic	8 thin ham slices
1½ teaspoons salt	4 small dill pickles, thinly sliced lengthwise
½ teaspoon crushed red pepper flakes	

1. Coat **CROCK-POT**® slow cooker with nonstick cooking spray. Add pork loin.

2. Combine orange juice, lime juice, garlic, salt and pepper flakes in small bowl. Pour over pork. Cover; cook on LOW 7 to 8 hours or on HIGH 3½ to 4 hours. Transfer pork to cutting board and allow to cool. Cut into thin slices.

3. To serve, spread mustard on both sides of rolls. Divide pork slices among roll bottoms. Top with Swiss cheese slice, ham slice and pickle slices. Cover with top of roll.

4. Coat large skillet with nonstick cooking spray and heat over medium heat until hot. Working in batches, arrange sandwiches in skillet. Cover with foil and top with dinner plate to press down sandwiches. (If necessary, weigh down with 2 to 3 cans to compress sandwiches lightly.) Heat until cheese is slightly melted, about 8 minutes.* Serve immediately.

Makes 8 servings

*Or use tabletop grill to compress and heat sandwiches.

PREP TIME: 20 minutes
COOK TIME: 7 to 8 hours (LOW) or 3½ to 4 hours (HIGH)

Mile-High Enchilada Pie

5 (6-inch) corn tortillas

1 jar (12 ounces) salsa

1 can (15½ ounces) kidney
   beans, rinsed and drained

1 cup shredded cooked chicken

1 cup (about 4 ounces)
   shredded Monterey Jack
   cheese with jalapeño
   peppers

Fresh cilantro and sliced red
   pepper (optional)

1. Prepare foil handles;* place in **CROCK-POT**® slow cooker. Place 1 tortilla on top of foil handles. Top with ¼ of the salsa, beans and chicken and ⅓ of cheese. Continue layering in order using remaining ingredients, ending with tortilla topped with last ¼ of cheese.

2. Cover; cook on LOW 6 to 8 hours or on HIGH 3 to 4 hours. Pull out by foil handles. Garnish with fresh cilantro and sliced red pepper, if desired.

Makes 4 to 6 servings

*To make foil handles, tear off three (18×2-inch) strips of heavy foil or use regular foil folded to double thickness. Crisscross foil strips in spoke design and place in **CROCK-POT**® slow cooker to make lifting tortilla stack easier.

PREP TIME: 20 minutes
COOK TIME: 6 to 8 hours (LOW) or 3 to 4 hours (HIGH)

Parmesan Potato Wedges

- 2 pounds red potatoes, cut into ½-inch wedges
- ¼ cup finely chopped yellow onion
- 1½ teaspoons dried oregano
- ½ teaspoon salt
- ¼ teaspoon black pepper, or to taste
- 2 tablespoons butter, cut into ⅛-inch pieces
- ¼ cup (1 ounce) grated Parmesan cheese

Layer potatoes, onion, oregano, salt, pepper and butter in **CROCK-POT**® slow cooker. Cover; cook on HIGH 4 hours. Transfer potatoes to serving platter and sprinkle with cheese.

Makes 6 servings

PREP TIME: 15 minutes
COOK TIME: 4 hours (HIGH)

Meatballs and Spaghetti Sauce

Meatballs

- **2** pounds 90% lean ground beef
- **1** cup bread crumbs
- **1** onion, chopped
- **2** eggs, beaten
- **¼** cup minced flat-leaf parsley
- **2** teaspoons minced garlic
- **½** teaspoon dry mustard
- **½** teaspoon black pepper
- Olive oil

Spaghetti Sauce

- **1** can (28 ounces) peeled whole tomatoes
- **½** cup chopped fresh basil
- **2** tablespoons olive oil
- **2** cloves garlic, or to taste, finely minced
- **1** teaspoon sugar
- Salt and black pepper, to taste
- Cooked spaghetti

1. Combine all meatball ingredients except oil. Form into walnut-sized balls. Heat oil in skillet over medium heat until hot. Sear meatballs on all sides, turning as they brown. Transfer to **CROCK-POT**® slow cooker.

2. Combine all sauce ingredients in medium bowl. Pour over meatballs, stirring to coat. Cover; cook on LOW 3 to 5 hours or on HIGH 2 to 4 hours.

3. Adjust seasonings, if desired. Serve over spaghetti.

Makes 6 to 8 servings

Tip: Recipe can be doubled for a 5-, 6- or 7-quart **CROCK-POT**® slow cooker.

PREP TIME: 20 minutes
COOK TIME: 3 to 5 hours (LOW) or 2 to 4 hours (HIGH)

Cornbread Stuffing with Sausage and Green Apples

- 1 package (16 ounces) honey cornbread mix, plus ingredients to prepare mix
- 2 cups cubed French bread
- 1½ pounds mild Italian sausage, casings removed
- 1 onion, finely chopped
- 1 green apple, peeled, cored and diced
- 2 stalks celery, finely chopped
- ¼ teaspoon dried sage
- ¼ teaspoon dried rosemary
- ¼ teaspoon dried thyme
- ½ teaspoon salt
- ¼ teaspoon black pepper
- 3 cups chicken broth
- 2 tablespoons fresh chopped parsley (optional)

1. Mix and bake cornbread according to package directions. When cool, cover with plastic wrap and set aside overnight.*

2. Coat **CROCK-POT**® slow cooker with nonstick cooking spray. Preheat oven to 350°F. Cut cornbread into 1-inch cubes. Spread cornbread and French bread on baking sheet. Toast in oven about 20 minutes or until dry.

3. Meanwhile, heat medium skillet over medium heat until hot. Add sausage. Cook and stir until browned. Transfer sausage to **CROCK-POT**® slow cooker with slotted spoon.

4. Add onion, apple and celery to skillet. Cook and stir 5 minutes or until softened. Stir in sage, rosemary, thyme, salt and pepper. Transfer mixture to **CROCK-POT**® slow cooker.

5. Add bread cubes and stir gently to combine. Pour broth over mixture. Cover; cook on HIGH 3 to 3½ hours or until liquid is absorbed. Garnish with parsley, if desired.

Makes 8 to 12 servings

*Or purchase prepared 8-inch square pan of cornbread. Proceed as directed.

PREP TIME: 35 to 45 minutes
COOK TIME: 3 to 3½ hours (HIGH)

Chicken Enchilada Roll-Ups

6 boneless, skinless chicken breasts (about 1½ pounds)

½ cup plus 2 tablespoons all-purpose flour, divided

½ teaspoon salt

2 tablespoons butter

1 cup chicken broth

1 small onion, diced

¼ to ½ cup canned jalapeño peppers, sliced

½ teaspoon dried oregano

2 tablespoons heavy cream or milk

6 (7- to 8-inch) flour tortillas

6 thin slices American cheese or American cheese with jalapeño peppers

1. Cut each chicken breast lengthwise into 2 or 3 strips. Combine ½ cup flour and salt in resealable plastic food storage bag. Add chicken strips and shake to coat with flour mixture. Melt butter in large skillet over medium heat. Brown chicken strips in batches, cooking 2 to 3 minutes per side. Transfer to **CROCK-POT**® slow cooker.

2. Add chicken broth to skillet and scrape up any browned bits. Pour broth mixture into **CROCK-POT**® slow cooker. Add onion, jalapeño peppers and oregano. Cover; cook on LOW 7 to 8 hours or on HIGH 3 to 4 hours.

3. Blend remaining 2 tablespoons flour and cream in small bowl until smooth. Stir into chicken mixture. Cook, uncovered, on HIGH 15 minutes or until thickened. Spoon chicken mixture onto center of flour tortillas. Top each with cheese slice. Fold up tortillas and serve.

Makes 6 servings

PREP TIME: 20 minutes
COOK TIME: 7¼ to 8¼ hours (LOW) or 3¼ to 4¼ hours (HIGH)

Bacon and Onion Brisket

6 slices bacon, cut crosswise into ½-inch strips

1 flat-cut boneless brisket, seasoned with salt and black pepper (about 2½ pounds)

3 medium onions, sliced

2 cans (10½ ounces each) condensed beef consommé, undiluted

1. Cook bacon strips in large skillet over medium-high heat about 3 minutes. Do not overcook. Transfer bacon with slotted spoon to **CROCK-POT®** slow cooker.

2. Sear brisket in hot bacon fat on all sides, turning as it browns. Transfer to **CROCK-POT®** slow cooker.

3. Lower skillet heat to medium. Add sliced onions to skillet. Cook and stir 3 to 5 minutes or until softened. Add to **CROCK-POT®** slow cooker. Pour in consommé. Cover; cook on HIGH 6 to 8 hours or until meat is tender.

4. Transfer brisket to cutting board and let rest 10 minutes. Slice brisket against the grain into thin slices, and arrange on platter. Add salt and pepper, if desired. Spoon bacon, onions and cooking liquid over brisket to serve.

Makes 6 servings

PREP TIME: 20 minutes
COOK TIME: 6 to 8 hours (HIGH)

Sweet 'N' Spicy Ribs

5 cups barbecue sauce	1 tablespoon garlic powder
¾ cup packed dark brown sugar	1 tablespoon onion powder
¼ cup honey	6 pounds pork or beef back ribs, cut into 3-rib portions
2 tablespoons Cajun seasoning	

1. Combine barbecue sauce, sugar, honey, Cajun seasoning, garlic powder and onion powder in medium bowl. Remove 1 cup mixture; refrigerate and reserve for dipping sauce.

2. Place ribs in large **CROCK-POT**® slow cooker. Pour barbecue sauce mixture over ribs. Cover; cook on LOW 8 hours or until meat is very tender.

3. Transfer ribs to serving platter; cover with foil to keep warm. Skim fat from sauce and discard. Serve ribs with additional reserved sauce.

Makes 10 servings

PREP TIME: 20 minutes
COOK TIME: 8 hours (LOW)

Beef Stew with Bacon, Onion and Sweet Potatoes

1 pound beef for stew, cut into 1-inch chunks

1 can (14½ ounces) beef broth

2 medium sweet potatoes, peeled and cut into 2-inch chunks

1 large onion, cut into 1½-inch chunks

2 slices thick-cut bacon, diced

1 teaspoon dried thyme

1 teaspoon salt

¼ teaspoon black pepper

2 tablespoons cornstarch

2 tablespoons water

1. Coat **CROCK-POT**® slow cooker with nonstick cooking spray. Combine all ingredients except cornstarch and water in **CROCK-POT**® slow cooker; mix well. Cover; cook on LOW 7 to 8 hours or on HIGH 4 to 5 hours, or until meat and vegetables are tender.

2. With slotted spoon, transfer beef and vegetables to serving bowl; cover with foil to keep warm.

3. Turn **CROCK-POT**® slow cooker to HIGH. Combine cornstarch and water; stir until smooth. Stir into cooking liquid. Cover; cook 15 minutes or until thickened. To serve, spoon sauce over beef and vegetables.

Makes 4 servings

PREP TIME: 10 minutes
COOK TIME: 7¼ to 8¼ hours (LOW) or 4¼ to 5¼ hours (HIGH)

Chorizo Burritos

15 ounces chorizo, cut into bite-size pieces

1 can (about 15 ounces) red beans, rinsed and drained

1 can (about 14 ounces) diced tomatoes

1 can (11 ounces) corn, drained

2 green or red bell peppers, cut into 1-inch pieces

1 cup chicken broth

½ teaspoon ground cumin

½ teaspoon ground cinnamon

8 to 10 flour tortillas, warmed

Hot cooked rice

Shredded Monterey Jack cheese or sour cream

1. Place all ingredients except tortillas, rice and cheese into **CROCK-POT®** slow cooker; mix well. Cover; cook on LOW 6 to 8 hours.

2. Spoon filling down centers of warm tortillas; top with rice and shredded cheese. Roll up and serve immediately.

Makes 5 to 6 servings

PREP TIME: 15 minutes
COOK TIME: 6 to 8 hours (LOW)

Chicken and Wild Rice Casserole

- 2 slices bacon, chopped
- 3 tablespoons olive oil
- 1½ pounds chicken thighs, trimmed of excess skin
- ½ cup diced onion
- ½ cup diced celery
- 2 tablespoons Worcestershire sauce
- ¾ teaspoon salt
- ¼ teaspoon black pepper
- ½ teaspoon dried sage
- 1 cup converted long-grain white rice
- 1 package (4 ounces) wild rice
- 6 ounces brown mushrooms, wiped clean and quartered*
- 3 cups hot chicken broth, or enough to cover chicken
- Salt and black pepper, to taste
- 2 tablespoons chopped parsley, for garnish

*Use "baby bellas" or crimini mushrooms. Or, you may substitute white button mushrooms.

1. Microwave bacon on HIGH (100% power) 1 minute. Transfer to **CROCK-POT®** slow cooker. Add olive oil and spread evenly on bottom. Place chicken in **CROCK-POT®** slow cooker, skin side down. Add remaining ingredients in order given, except parsley. Cover; cook on LOW 3 to 4 hours, or until rice is tender.

2. Uncover and let stand 15 minutes. Add salt and pepper, if desired. Remove skin before serving, if desired. Garnish with chopped parsley.

Makes 4 to 6 servings

PREP TIME: 15 minutes
COOK TIME: 3 to 4 hours (LOW)

No-Fuss Macaroni & Cheese

2 cups (about 8 ounces) uncooked elbow macaroni

4 ounces light pasteurized processed cheese, cubed

1 cup (4 ounces) shredded mild Cheddar cheese

½ teaspoon salt

⅛ teaspoon black pepper

1½ cups fat-free (skim) milk

Combine macaroni, cheeses, salt and pepper in **CROCK-POT**® slow cooker. Pour milk over all. Cover; cook on LOW 2 to 3 hours, stirring after 20 to 30 minutes.

Makes 6 to 8 servings

PREP TIME: 10 minutes
COOK TIME: 2 to 3 hours (LOW)

Barbecued Pulled Pork Sandwiches

1 pork shoulder roast
  (2½ pounds)

1 bottle (14 ounces) barbecue
  sauce

1 tablespoon fresh lemon juice

1 teaspoon packed brown sugar

1 medium onion, chopped

8 hamburger buns or hard rolls

1. Place pork roast in **CROCK-POT**® slow cooker. Cover; cook on LOW 8 to 10 hours or on HIGH 4 to 5 hours.

2. Remove pork roast from **CROCK-POT**®. Shred with two forks. Discard cooking liquid. Return pork to **CROCK-POT**®; add barbecue sauce, lemon juice, sugar and onion. Cover and cook on LOW 2 hours or on HIGH 1 hour. Serve pork on hamburger buns or hard rolls.

Makes 8 servings

Note: This kid-popular dish is sweet and savory, and most importantly, extremely easy to make. Serve with crunchy coleslaw on the side.

Tip: For a 5-, 6- or 7-quart **CROCK-POT**® slow cooker, double all ingredients, except for the barbecue sauce. Increase the barbecue sauce to 21 ounces (or about 1½ bottles).

PREP TIME: 15 to 20 minutes
COOK TIME: 10 to 12 hours (LOW) or 5 to 6 hours (HIGH)

Fantastic *Finishes*

Streusel Pound Cake

1 package (16 ounces) pound cake mix, plus ingredients to prepare mix
¼ cup packed light brown sugar
1 tablespoon all-purpose flour
¼ cup chopped nuts
1 teaspoon ground cinnamon
Strawberries, blueberries, raspberries and/or powdered sugar (optional)

Coat 4½-quart **CROCK-POT**® slow cooker with nonstick cooking spray. Prepare cake mix according to package directions; stir in brown sugar, flour, nuts and cinnamon. Pour batter into **CROCK-POT**® slow cooker. Cover; cook on HIGH 1½ to 1¾ hours or until toothpick inserted into center of cake comes out clean. Serve with berries and powdered sugar, if desired.

Makes 6 to 8 servings

PREP TIME: 10 to 15 minutes
COOK TIME: 1½ to 1¾ hours (HIGH)

S'Mores Fondue

1 pound milk chocolate, chopped

2 jars (7 ounces each) marshmallow creme

⅔ cup half-and-half

2 teaspoons vanilla

4 bananas

1 cup mini marshmallows

24 graham crackers

24 strawberries

1. Combine chocolate, marshmallow creme, half-and-half and vanilla in **CROCK-POT®** slow cooker. Cover and cook on LOW 1½ to 3 hours, stirring after 1 hour.

2. Meanwhile, peel bananas and cut into ½-inch slices. Sprinkle top of fondue dip with mini marshmallows and serve with banana slices, graham crackers and strawberries.

Makes 8 to 12 servings

PREP TIME: 15 minutes
COOK TIME: 1½ to 3 hours (LOW)

Chai Tea

2 quarts (8 cups) water
8 bags black tea
¾ cup sugar*
16 whole cloves
16 whole cardamom seeds, pods removed (optional)

5 cinnamon sticks
8 slices fresh ginger
1 cup milk

*Chai tea is typically sweet. For less-sweet tea, reduce sugar to ½ cup.

1. Combine water, tea, sugar, cloves, cardamom, if desired, cinnamon and ginger in **CROCK-POT**® slow cooker. Cover; cook on HIGH 2 to 2½ hours.

2. Strain mixture; discard solids. (At this point, tea may be covered and refrigerated up to 3 days.)

3. Stir in milk just before serving. Serve warm or chilled.

Makes 8 to 10 servings

PREP TIME: 5 minutes
COOK TIME: 2 to 2½ hours (HIGH)

Fantastic Finishes

Mixed Berry Cobbler

1 package (16 ounces) frozen mixed berries

¾ cup granulated sugar

2 tablespoons quick-cooking tapioca

2 teaspoons grated lemon peel

1½ cups all-purpose flour

½ cup packed light brown sugar

2¼ teaspoons baking powder

¼ teaspoon ground nutmeg

¾ cup milk

⅓ cup butter, melted

Vanilla ice cream or whipped cream (optional)

1. Coat **CROCK-POT**® slow cooker with nonstick cooking spray. Stir together berries, granulated sugar, tapioca and lemon peel in medium bowl. Transfer to **CROCK-POT**® slow cooker.

2. For topping, combine flour, brown sugar, baking powder and nutmeg in medium bowl. Add milk and butter; stir just until blended. Drop spoonfuls of dough on top of berry mixture. Cover; cook on LOW 4 hours. Uncover; let stand about 30 minutes. Serve with ice cream, if desired.

Makes 8 servings

Tip: Cobblers are year-round favorites. Experiment with seasonal fresh fruits, such as pears, plums, peaches, rhubarb, blueberries, raspberries, strawberries, blackberries or gooseberries. Try different apple varieties, including newer ones such as Pink Lady, or a blend of your favorite apples to come up with your own signature cobbler.

PREP TIME: 15 minutes
COOK TIME: 4½ hours (LOW)

Homestyle Apple Brown Betty

6   cups of your favorite cooking apples, peeled, cored and cut into eighths

1   cup bread crumbs

1   teaspoon ground cinnamon

1   teaspoon ground nutmeg

⅛   teaspoon salt

¾   cup packed brown sugar

½   cup (1 stick) butter or margarine, melted

¼   cup finely chopped walnuts

1. Lightly grease **CROCK-POT**® slow cooker. Place apples on bottom.

2. Combine bread crumbs, cinnamon, nutmeg, salt, sugar, butter and walnuts. Spread over apples.

3. Cover; cook on LOW 3 to 4 hours or on HIGH 2 hours.

Makes 8 servings

Note: This recipe conjures up an amazing dessert out of simple ingredients.

Tip: Recipe can be doubled for a 5-, 6- or 7-quart **CROCK-POT**® slow cooker.

PREP TIME: 15 minutes
COOK TIME: 3 to 4 hours (LOW) or 2 hours (HIGH)

Fantastic Finishes

Chocolate Hazelnut Pudding Cake

1 box (18¼ ounces) golden yellow cake mix

1 cup water

4 eggs

½ cup sour cream

½ cup vegetable oil

1 cup mini semisweet chocolate chips

½ cup chopped hazelnuts

Whipped cream or ice cream (optional)

1. Coat 6-quart **CROCK-POT**® slow cooker with nonstick cooking spray. Combine cake mix, water, eggs, sour cream and oil; mix smooth. Pour batter into **CROCK-POT**® slow cooker. Cover; cook on HIGH 2 hours, or until batter is nearly set.

2. Sprinkle on mini chocolate chips and hazelnuts. Cover; cook on HIGH 30 minutes longer, or until toothpick inserted into center comes out clean or cake begins to pull away from sides of **CROCK-POT**® slow cooker. Let stand until cool and slice, or spoon out while warm. Serve with whipped cream, if desired.

Makes 10 servings

PREP TIME: 5 minutes
COOK TIME: 2½ hours (HIGH)

Pineapple Daiquiri Sundae Topping

1 pineapple, peeled, cored and cut into ½-inch chunks

½ cup dark rum

½ cup sugar

3 tablespoons lime juice

Peel of 2 limes, cut in long strips

1 tablespoon cornstarch

Ice cream, pound cake or shortcake

Fresh raspberries and mint leaves (optional)

Place pineapple, rum, sugar, lime juice, lime peel and cornstarch in 1½-quart **CROCK-POT**® slow cooker; mix well. Cover; cook on HIGH 3 to 4 hours. Serve hot over ice cream, pound cake or shortcake. Top with raspberries and mint leaves, if desired.

Makes 4 to 6 servings

Variation: Substitute 1 can (20 ounces) crushed pineapple, drained, for the fresh pineapple. Cook on HIGH 3 hours.

PREP TIME: 5 minutes
COOK TIME: 3 to 4 hours (HIGH)

Baked Fudge Pudding Cake

6 tablespoons unsweetened cocoa powder

¼ cup all-purpose flour

⅛ teaspoon salt

4 eggs

1⅓ cups sugar

1 cup (2 sticks) unsalted butter, melted

1 teaspoon vanilla

Grated peel of 1 orange

½ cup whipping cream

Chopped toasted pecans

Whipped cream or vanilla ice cream

1. Coat 4½-quart **CROCK-POT®** slow cooker with nonstick cooking spray. Preheat **CROCK-POT®** slow cooker on LOW. Blend cocoa, flour and salt in small bowl; set aside.

2. Beat eggs in large bowl with electric mixer on medium-high speed until thickened. Gradually add sugar, beating about 5 minutes or until very thick and pale yellow. Mix in butter, vanilla and peel. Stir cocoa mixture into egg mixture. Add cream; mix until blended. Pour batter into **CROCK-POT®** slow cooker.

3. Cover opening of **CROCK-POT®** slow cooker with paper towel to collect condensation, making sure it doesn't touch batter. Place lid over paper towel. Cook on LOW 3 to 4 hours (do not cook on HIGH).

4. To serve, spoon into dishes. Sprinkle with toasted pecans, and top with whipped cream. Refrigerate leftovers.

Makes 6 to 8 servings

Tip: Refrigerate leftover pudding cake in a covered container. To serve warm, reheat individual servings in the microwave for about 15 seconds. Or, make fudge truffles.

PREP TIME: 15 minutes
COOK TIME: 3 to 4 hours (LOW)

Hot Tropics Sipper

4 cups pineapple juice

2 cups apple juice

1 container (about 11 ounces) apricot nectar

3 whole cinnamon sticks

6 whole cloves

½ cup packed dark brown sugar

1 medium lemon, thinly sliced

1 medium orange, thinly sliced

Additional lemon or orange slices, for garnish

Place all ingredients except garnish in **CROCK-POT®** slow cooker. Cover; cook on HIGH 3½ to 4 hours, or until very fragrant. Strain immediately (beverage will turn bitter if fruit and spices soak for too long after cooking is complete). Serve with fresh slices of lemon or orange, if desired.

Makes 8 servings

PREP TIME: 5 minutes
COOK TIME: 3½ to 4 hours (HIGH)

Spiced Plums and Pears

2 cans (29 ounces each) sliced
   pears in heavy syrup,
   undrained
2 pounds black or red plums
   (about 12 to 14), pitted and
   sliced
1 cup packed light brown sugar
1 teaspoon ground cinnamon

½ teaspoon ground ginger
¼ teaspoon grated lemon peel
2 tablespoons cornstarch
2 tablespoons water
   Pound cake or ice cream
   Whipped topping

1. Cut pear slices in half with spoon. Place pears, plums, sugar, cinnamon, ginger and lemon peel in **CROCK-POT**® slow cooker. Cover; cook on HIGH 4 hours.

2. Combine cornstarch and water to make smooth paste. Stir into fruit mixture. Cook on HIGH until slightly thickened.

3. Serve warm or at room temperature over pound cake with whipped topping.

Makes 6 to 8 servings

Tip: When adapting conventionally prepared recipes for your **CROCK-POT**® slow cooker, revise the amount of spices you use. For example, whole spices increase in flavor while ground spices tend to lose flavor during slow cooking. If you prefer, you can adjust the seasonings or add spices just before serving the dish.

PREP TIME: **15 minutes**
COOK TIME: **4 hours (HIGH)**

Decadent Chocolate Delight

1 **package (about 18 ounces) chocolate cake mix**

1 **container (8 ounces) sour cream**

1 **cup semisweet chocolate chips**

1 **cup water**

4 **eggs**

¾ **cup vegetable oil**

1 **package (4-serving size) instant chocolate pudding and pie filling mix**

Vanilla ice cream

1. Coat 4½-quart **CROCK-POT**® slow cooker with nonstick cooking spray.

2. Combine all ingredients except ice cream in medium bowl; mix well. Transfer to **CROCK-POT**® slow cooker.

3. Cover; cook on LOW 3 to 4 hours or on HIGH 1½ to 1¾ hours. Serve hot or warm with ice cream.

Makes 12 servings

PREP TIME: **10 minutes**
COOK TIME: 3 to 4 hours (LOW) or 1½ to 1¾ hours (HIGH)

Pineapple Rice Pudding

1 can (20 ounces) crushed pineapple in juice, undrained

1 can (13½ ounces) coconut milk

1 can (12 ounces) fat-free evaporated milk

¾ cup uncooked arborio rice

2 eggs, lightly beaten

¼ cup granulated sugar

¼ cup packed light brown sugar

½ teaspoon ground cinnamon

¼ teaspoon ground nutmeg

¼ teaspoon salt

Toasted coconut* and pineapple slices (optional)

*To toast coconut, spread evenly on ungreased baking sheet. Toast in preheated 350°F oven 5 to 7 minutes, stirring occasionally, until light golden brown.

1. Place pineapple with juice, coconut milk, evaporated milk, rice, eggs, granulated sugar, brown sugar, cinnamon, nutmeg and salt into **CROCK-POT**® slow cooker; mix well. Cover; cook on HIGH 3 to 4 hours or until thickened and rice is tender.

2. Stir until blended. Serve warm or chilled. Garnish with coconut and pineapple, if desired.

Makes 8 servings

PREP TIME: 10 minutes
COOK TIME: 3 to 4 hours (HIGH)

Fantastic Finishes

Brioche and Amber Rum Custard

2 tablespoons unsalted butter
3½ cups heavy cream
4 large eggs
½ cup packed dark brown sugar
⅓ cup amber or light rum
2 teaspoons vanilla

1 loaf (20 to 22 ounces) brioche bread, torn into pieces or 5 large brioche, cut into thirds*
½ cup coarsely chopped pecans
Caramel or butterscotch topping (optional)

*If desired, trim and discard heels.

1. Generously coat **CROCK-POT**® slow cooker with butter. Combine cream, eggs, sugar, rum and vanilla in large bowl. Stir well to combine.

2. Mound one fourth of brioche pieces in bottom of prepared **CROCK-POT**® slow cooker. Ladle one fourth of cream mixture over brioche. Sprinkle with one third of pecans. Repeat layers with remaining brioche, cream mixture and nuts.

3. Cover; cook on LOW 3 to 3½ hours or on HIGH 1¾ to 2 hours. Continue cooking until custard is set and tester inserted into center comes out clean.

4. Serve warm. Drizzle with caramel topping, if desired.

Makes 4 to 6 servings

PREP TIME: 15 minutes
COOK TIME: 3 to 3½ hours (LOW) or 1¾ to 2 hours (HIGH)

Triple Chocolate Fantasy

2 pounds white almond bark, broken into pieces

1 bar (4 ounces) sweetened chocolate, broken into pieces*

1 package (12 ounces) semisweet chocolate chips

3 cups lightly toasted, coarsely chopped pecans**

*Use your favorite high-quality chocolate candy bar.

**To toast pecans, spread in single layer on baking sheet. Bake in preheated 350°F oven 8 to 10 minutes or until golden brown, stirring frequently.

1. Place bark, sweetened chocolate and chocolate chips in **CROCK-POT**® slow cooker. Cover; cook on HIGH 1 hour. Do not stir.

2. Turn **CROCK-POT**® slow cooker to LOW. Continue cooking 1 hour, stirring every 15 minutes. Stir in nuts.

3. Drop mixture by tablespoonfuls onto baking sheet covered with waxed paper; let cool. Store in tightly covered container.

Makes 36 pieces

Variations: Here are a few ideas for other imaginative items to add in along with or instead of pecans: raisins, crushed peppermint candy, candy-coated baking bits, crushed toffee, peanuts or pistachios, chopped gum drops, chopped dried fruit, candied cherries, chopped marshmallows or sweetened coconut.

PREP TIME: 10 minutes
COOK TIME: 1 hour (HIGH) plus 1 hour (LOW)

Coconut Rice Pudding

2 cups water
1 cup uncooked converted long-grain rice
1 tablespoon unsalted butter
Pinch salt
2¼ cups evaporated milk
1 can (14 ounces) cream of coconut

½ cup golden raisins
3 egg yolks, beaten
Grated peel of 2 limes
1 teaspoon vanilla
Toasted shredded coconut (optional)

1. Place water, rice, butter and salt in medium saucepan. Bring to a boil over high heat, stirring frequently. Reduce heat to low. Cover; cook 10 to 12 minutes. Remove from heat. Let stand, covered, 5 minutes.

2. Meanwhile, coat **CROCK-POT**® slow cooker with nonstick cooking spray. Add evaporated milk, cream of coconut, raisins, egg yolks, lime peel and vanilla; mix well. Add rice; stir until blended.

3. Cover; cook on LOW 4 hours or on HIGH 2 hours. Stir every 30 minutes, if possible. Pudding will thicken as it cools. Garnish with toasted shredded coconut, if desired.

Makes 6 servings

PREP TIME: 25 minutes

COOK TIME: 4 hours (LOW) or 2 hours (HIGH)

Strawberry Rhubarb Crisp

Fruit

- **4 cups sliced hulled strawberries**
- **4 cups diced rhubarb (about 5 stalks), cut into ½-inch dice**
- **1½ cups granulated sugar**
- **2 tablespoons lemon juice**
- **1½ tablespoons cornstarch, plus water (optional)**

Topping

- **1 cup all-purpose flour**
- **1 cup old-fashioned oats**
- **½ cup granulated sugar**
- **½ cup packed brown sugar**
- **½ teaspoon ground ginger**
- **½ teaspoon ground nutmeg**
- **½ cup (1 stick) butter, cut into pieces**
- **½ cup sliced almonds, toasted***

*To toast almonds, spread in single layer on baking sheet. Bake in preheated 350°F oven 8 to 10 minutes or until golden brown, stirring frequently.

1. Prepare fruit. Coat **CROCK-POT**® slow cooker with nonstick cooking spray. Place strawberries, rhubarb, granulated sugar and lemon juice in **CROCK-POT**® slow cooker and mix well. Cook on HIGH 1½ hours or until fruit is tender.

2. If fruit is dry after cooking, add a little water. If fruit has too much liquid, mix cornstarch with a small amount of water and stir into fruit. Cook on HIGH an additional 15 minutes or until cooking liquid is thickened.

3. Preheat oven to 375°F. Prepare topping. Combine flour, oats, sugars, ginger and nutmeg in medium bowl. Cut in butter using pastry cutter or 2 knives until mixture resembles coarse crumbs. Stir in almonds.

4. Remove lid from **CROCK-POT**® slow cooker and gently sprinkle topping onto fruit. Transfer stoneware to oven. Bake 15 to 20 minutes or until topping begins to brown.

Makes 8 servings

PREP TIME: **20 minutes**
COOK TIME: **1½ to 1¾ hours (HIGH)**

Fresh Berry Compote

2 cups fresh blueberries

4 cups fresh sliced strawberries

2 tablespoons orange juice

½ to ¾ cup sugar

4 slices (½ × 1½ inches) lemon peel with no white pith

1 cinnamon stick or ½ teaspoon ground cinnamon

1. Place blueberries in **CROCK-POT®** slow cooker. Cover; cook on HIGH 45 minutes until blueberries begin to soften.

2. Add strawberries, orange juice, ½ cup sugar, lemon peel and cinnamon stick. Stir to blend. Cover; cook on HIGH 1 to 1½ hours or until berries soften and sugar dissolves. Check for sweetness and add more sugar if necessary, cooking until added sugar dissolves.

3. Remove insert from **CROCK-POT** slow cooker to heatproof surface and let cool. Serve compote warm or chilled.

Makes 4 servings

Tip: To turn this compote into a fresh-fruit topping for cake, ice cream, waffles or pancakes, carefully spoon out fruit, leaving cooking liquid in **CROCK-POT®** slow cooker. Blend 1 to 2 tablespoons cornstarch with ¼ cup cold water until smooth. Add to cooking liquid and cook on HIGH until thickened. Return fruit to sauce and blend in gently.

PREP TIME: 5 minutes
COOK TIME: 1¾ to 2¼ hours (HIGH)

Orange Cranberry-Nut Bread

2 cups all-purpose flour	2 teaspoons dried orange peel
1 teaspoon baking powder	⅔ cup boiling water
½ teaspoon baking soda	¾ cup sugar
¼ teaspoon salt	2 tablespoons shortening
½ cup chopped pecans	1 egg, lightly beaten
1 cup dried cranberries	1 teaspoon vanilla

1. Coat 3-quart **CROCK-POT**® slow cooker with nonstick cooking spray. Blend flour, baking powder, baking soda and salt in medium bowl. Mix in pecans; set aside.

2. Combine cranberries and orange peel in separate medium bowl; pour boiling water over fruit mixture and stir. Add sugar, shortening, egg and vanilla; stir just until blended. Add flour mixture; stir just until blended.

3. Pour batter into **CROCK-POT**® slow cooker. Cover; cook on HIGH 1¼ to 1½ hours or until edges begin to brown and cake tester inserted into center comes out clean. Remove stoneware from **CROCK-POT**® slow cooker. Cool on wire rack about 10 minutes; remove bread from stoneware and cool completely on rack.

Makes 8 to 10 servings

Tip: This recipe works best in round **CROCK-POT**® slow cookers.

PREP TIME: **10 minutes**
COOK TIME: **1¼ to 1½ hours (HIGH)**

Pecan-Cinnamon Pudding Cake

1⅓ cups all-purpose flour
½ cup granulated sugar
1½ teaspoons baking powder
1½ teaspoons ground cinnamon
⅔ cup milk

5 tablespoons butter or margarine, melted, divided
1 cup chopped pecans
1½ cups water
¾ cup packed brown sugar
Whipped cream (optional)

1. Coat 4½-quart **CROCK-POT**® slow cooker with nonstick cooking spray or butter. Combine flour, granulated sugar, baking powder and cinnamon in medium bowl. Add milk and 3 tablespoons butter; mix just until blended. Stir in pecans. Spread on bottom of **CROCK-POT**® slow cooker.

2. Combine water, brown sugar, and remaining 2 tablespoons butter in small saucepan; bring to a boil. Pour over batter in **CROCK-POT**® slow cooker. Do not stir.

3. Cover; cook on HIGH 1¼ to 1½ hours or until toothpick inserted into center comes out clean. Let stand, uncovered, for 30 minutes, then invert onto serving plate. Serve warm with whipped cream, if desired.

Makes 8 servings

PREP TIME: 10 minutes
COOK TIME: 1¼ to 1½ hours (HIGH)

Bananas Foster

12 bananas, cut into quarters

1 cup flaked coconut

1 teaspoon ground cinnamon

½ teaspoon salt

1 cup dark corn syrup

⅔ cup butter, melted

2 teaspoons grated lemon peel

¼ cup lemon juice

2 teaspoons rum

12 slices pound cake

1 quart vanilla ice cream

Combine bananas and coconut in **CROCK-POT**® slow cooker. Combine cinnamon, salt, corn syrup, butter, lemon peel, lemon juice and rum in medium bowl; pour over bananas. Cover; cook on LOW 1 to 2 hours. To serve, arrange bananas on pound cake slices. Top with ice cream and pour on warm sauce.

Makes 12 servings

PREP TIME: 5 to 10 minutes
COOK TIME: 1 to 2 hours (LOW)

Mulled Cranberry Tea

2 tea bags
1 cup boiling water
1 bottle (48 ounces) cranberry juice
½ cup dried cranberries (optional)
⅓ cup sugar

1 large lemon, cut into ¼-inch slices
4 cinnamon sticks
6 whole cloves
   Additional cinnamon sticks and thin lemon slices (optional)

1. Place tea bags in **CROCK-POT**® slow cooker. Pour boiling water over tea bags; cover and let steep 5 minutes. Remove and discard tea bags.

2. Stir in cranberry juice, cranberries, if desired, sugar, lemon slices, 4 cinnamon sticks and cloves. Cover; cook on LOW 2 to 3 hours or on HIGH 1 to 2 hours.

3. Remove and discard cooked lemon slices, cinnamon sticks and cloves. Serve in warm mug with cinnamon stick or fresh lemon slice, if desired.

Makes 8 servings

Tip: The flavor and aroma of crushed or ground herbs and spices may lessen during a longer cooking time. So, for slow cooking in your **CROCK-POT**® slow cooker, you may use whole herbs and spices. Be sure to taste and adjust your seasonings before serving.

PREP TIME: 10 minutes
COOK TIME: 2 to 3 hours (LOW) or 1 to 2 hours (HIGH)

Easy Chocolate Pudding Cake

1 package (6-serving size) instant chocolate pudding and pie filling mix

3 cups milk

1 package (about 18 ounces) chocolate fudge cake mix, plus ingredients to prepare mix

Crushed peppermint candies (optional)

Whipped topping or ice cream (optional)

1. Coat 4-quart **CROCK-POT**® slow cooker with nonstick cooking spray. Place pudding mix in **CROCK-POT**® slow cooker. Whisk in milk.

2. Prepare cake mix according to package directions. Carefully pour cake mix into **CROCK-POT**® slow cooker. Do not stir. Cover; cook on HIGH 1½ hours or until cake tester inserted into center comes out clean.

3. Spoon into cup or onto plate; serve warm with crushed peppermint candies and whipped topping, if desired.

Makes 16 servings

Tip: Allow breads, cakes and puddings to cool at least 5 minutes before scooping or removing them from the **CROCK-POT**® stoneware.

PREP TIME: 15 minutes
COOK TIME: 1½ hours (HIGH)

Cinnamon Latté

6 cups double-strength brewed coffee*

2 cups half-and-half

1 cup sugar

1 teaspoon vanilla

3 cinnamon sticks, plus additional for garnish

Whipped cream (optional)

*Double the amount of coffee grounds normally used to brew coffee. Or, substitute 8 teaspoons instant coffee dissolved in 6 cups boiling water.

1. Blend coffee, half-and-half, sugar and vanilla in 3- to 4-quart **CROCK-POT**® slow cooker. Add cinnamon sticks. Cover; cook on HIGH 3 hours.

2. Remove cinnamon sticks. Serve latté in tall coffee mugs with dollop of whipped cream and cinnamon stick, if desired.

Makes 6 to 8 servings

PREP TIME: 5 minutes
COOK TIME: 3 hours (HIGH)

Banana Nut Bread

⅓ cup butter or margarine	1¾ cups all-purpose flour
⅔ cup sugar	2 teaspoons baking powder
2 eggs, well beaten	½ teaspoon salt
2 tablespoons dark corn syrup	¼ teaspoon baking soda
3 ripe bananas, well mashed	½ cup chopped walnuts

1. Grease and flour inside of **CROCK-POT**® slow cooker. Cream butter in large bowl with electric mixer until fluffy. Slowly add sugar, eggs, corn syrup and mashed bananas. Beat until smooth.

2. Sift together flour, baking powder, salt and baking soda in small bowl. Slowly beat flour mixture into creamed mixture. Add walnuts and mix thoroughly. Pour into **CROCK-POT**® slow cooker. Cover; cook on HIGH 2 to 3 hours.

3. Let cool, then turn bread out onto serving platter.

Makes 6 servings

Note: Banana nut bread has always been a favorite way to use up those overripe bananas. Not only is it delicious, but it also freezes well for future use.

Tip: Recipe can be doubled for a 5-, 6- or 7-quart **CROCK-POT**® slow cooker.

PREP TIME: 15 minutes
COOK TIME: 2 to 3 hours (HIGH)

Index

Index

252

METRIC CONVERSION CHART

VOLUME MEASUREMENTS (dry)

$^1/_8$ teaspoon = 0.5 mL
$^1/_4$ teaspoon = 1 mL
$^1/_2$ teaspoon = 2 mL
$^3/_4$ teaspoon = 4 mL
1 teaspoon = 5 mL
1 tablespoon = 15 mL
2 tablespoons = 30 mL
$^1/_4$ cup = 60 mL
$^1/_3$ cup = 75 mL
$^1/_2$ cup = 125 mL
$^2/_3$ cup = 150 mL
$^3/_4$ cup = 175 mL
1 cup = 250 mL
2 cups = 1 pint = 500 mL
3 cups = 750 mL
4 cups = 1 quart = 1 L

VOLUME MEASUREMENTS (fluid)

1 fluid ounce (2 tablespoons) = 30 mL
4 fluid ounces ($^1/_2$ cup) = 125 mL
8 fluid ounces (1 cup) = 250 mL
12 fluid ounces (1$^1/_2$ cups) = 375 mL
16 fluid ounces (2 cups) = 500 mL

WEIGHTS (mass)

$^1/_2$ ounce = 15 g
1 ounce = 30 g
3 ounces = 90 g
4 ounces = 120 g
8 ounces = 225 g
10 ounces = 285 g
12 ounces = 360 g
16 ounces = 1 pound = 450 g

DIMENSIONS

$^1/_{16}$ inch = 2 mm
$^1/_8$ inch = 3 mm
$^1/_4$ inch = 6 mm
$^1/_2$ inch = 1.5 cm
$^3/_4$ inch = 2 cm
1 inch = 2.5 cm

OVEN TEMPERATURES

250°F = 120°C
275°F = 140°C
300°F = 150°C
325°F = 160°C
350°F = 180°C
375°F = 190°C
400°F = 200°C
425°F = 220°C
450°F = 230°C

BAKING PAN SIZES

Utensil	Size in Inches/Quarts	Metric Volume	Size in Centimeters
Baking or Cake Pan (square or rectangular)	8×8×2	2 L	20×20×5
	9×9×2	2.5 L	23×23×5
	12×8×2	3 L	30×20×5
	13×9×2	3.5 L	33×23×5
Loaf Pan	8×4×3	1.5 L	20×10×7
	9×5×3	2 L	23×13×7
Round Layer Cake Pan	8×1½	1.2 L	20×4
	9×1½	1.5 L	23×4
Pie Plate	8×1¼	750 mL	20×3
	9×1¼	1 L	23×3
Baking Dish or Casserole	1 quart	1 L	—
	1½ quarts	1.5 L	—
	2 quarts	2 L	—